ENDORSEMENTS

"When the presence of God comes, the supernatural takes place. Every believer—regardless of their age, background, or credentials—is a temple of the Holy Spirit and has a call on their life to be a carrier of God's glory. In *Carriers of the Ark*, Andrew Hopkins takes you on a journey of hosting the Holy Spirit and spreading Kingdom impact as you hunger for more of God in your life. Solid biblical teaching and personal testimonies will help equip you to walk into your God-given calling with His love and His power. This book offers practical steps to activate these truths in your sphere of influence and to go deeper in your relationship with the Lord."

Dr. Ché Ahn
Founder and President, Harvest International Ministry
Founding and Senior Pastor, Harvest Rock Church, Pasadena, CA
International Chancellor, Wagner University
Founder, Ché Ahn Ministries

"As a former worship leader and forever worshipper, I love passionate worship that is biblically sound. Sadly, in much of the worship presented today, though the music is good (sometimes difficult to sing along to) and the lyrics often catchy, they rarely edify the believer towards a deeper walk with God, greater intimacy with the Lord, and deeper love for our neighbor. Andrew Hopkins is a rare exception…and an exceptional one at that. His deepest desire is to assist men and women to experience the presence of God in great measure, see the Lord's healing and restoration released in worship, and is fully committed to a lifestyle of worship grounded on the Word of God.

In the book *Carriers of the Ark*, Andrew Hopkins presents a balanced, practical, and dynamic view of the lifestyle of worship and its true effect on committed believers. It is written with many practical illustrations of what a truly dedicated (but non-religious) life that carries the Presence of God is to be like. I like the book so well, we plan to use it as a text for a future course at Vision. It is my hope that every believer that reads this excellent work will indeed become a carrier of the Presence of God, a carrier of the ark."

Stan E. DeKoven, Ph.D., MFT
President, Vision International University

"I can truly say Andrew Hopkins' book, *Carriers of The Ark,* is one of the most challenging, life-changing books I have ever read. As the priests of the Old Testament carried the Ark (the Presence of God) with poles on their shoulders, we too, were created to carry the awesome, overwhelming Presence and glory of God everywhere we go.

With each page of this book you will find yourself moving into greater dimensions of God's glory, causing your life and the lives of others to be changed forever. Even as we read in The Book of Acts about people's lives being healed and transformed by the passing shadow of Peter, you will discover how you too can be a "carrier" of that same awesome, life-changing, overwhelming glory and Presence of God - with signs, wonders and miracles being an ever-present part of your daily life and ministry."

Dr. A.L. "Papa" Gill
Best selling author, *God's Promises For Your Every Need*
International Apostolic Leader

"My friend, Andrew Hopkins is a revivalist, who happens to be a worship leader. He carries the same fire and mantle of some of the greats of the past who ignited awakenings. I always look for materials and books written by those who walk in the dynamics of what they proclaim.

Andrew's new book takes you on a journey of retrieving a legacy and faith, handed down once and for all....an authentic Book of Acts lifestyle of exploits and character. To be able to carry the Ark of His Presence is the greatest privilege that anyone can possess; it the one thing that will go on for eternity."

Sean Smith
Author, *Prophetic Evangelism* & *I Am Your Sign*
@revseansmith
www.seansmithministries.org

"Andrew has lived out the pages in this book for years. What you will read will inspire you to not only be a carrier of the Ark, but also to sustain God's presence through the seasons of life. This book will stir up passion for His presence in young and old alike.

One of the first things that impressed me about Andrew before he ever served in any capacity was his hunger for God and his desire to know the Word. Andrew led worship for years not just to bring a point of visitation for God in our church, but to create a place of habitation for the people of Summit to enjoy His presence.

This book in like manner will help you to become a carrier, as you enjoy His daily presence and bring it to a thirsty world. *Carriers of the Ark* is full of fresh revelation that will help transform your life and those you come in contact with. We love Andrew & Rochelle and commend Breaker Ministries for any church or conference that wants to host the Presence."

Daniel & Theresa Jones
Apostolic Leaders, Senior Pastors
Summit Church, San Marcos, CA

"I first met Andrew at the Fire and Glory Outpouring in San Diego. In my travels, I encounter hundreds of worship leaders and styles yet very few like Andrew. As he began to lead worship, I knew something was different, but what? I was instantly ushered into the Presence of the Lord, one hour felt like 30 minutes, and when it was my time to speak, I wished we could've stayed in worship longer.

What makes Andrew Hopkins different? He is living the content found in this book. *Carriers of the Ark* isn't a book about techniques on how to enter God's Presence, but rather the character and inner life that attracts the Presence of the Lord. Is it biblical to "attract" the Presence?

> *"Thus says the LORD, "Heaven is My throne and the earth is My footstool. Where then is a house you could build for Me? And where is a place that I may rest? For My hand made all these things, Thus all these things came into being," declares the LORD. "But to this one I will look, To him who is humble and contrite of spirit, and who trembles at My word."*
>
> *Isaiah 66:1-2 NASB*

God rests upon those who are humble, contrite, and tremble at His word! In the pages of this book, you will discover truths of living a life worthy of God resting upon."

Ivan Roman
Senior Leader, Empowered Life Church, Medford, OR
Author, *Prophets Among Us*

CARRIERS

of the

ARK

**WHAT GOD WANTS TO FORM
IN YOU SO YOU CAN CARRY MORE
OF HIM UPON YOU**

ANDREW HOPKINS

Published by Breaker Ministries

Cover design by Josh Minor, Minor Design & Co. and Andrew Hopkins

ISBN: 978-0-578-67261-8

ISBN eBook: 978-0-578-67262-5

ACKNOWLEDGEMENTS

I would like to take a moment to thank those who've been supportive through not only the writing of this book, but also those who've walked with me through highs and lows and have provided contexts for the content of this book to come alive in.

My beautiful wife, Rochelle. Thank you for always believing in me, supporting and encouraging me. You've been an anchor in my life. You really live up to your name "little rock". I love you Huns and I'm proud to be your husband.

Jerame & Miranda Nelson - Thanks for taking me under your wing! I've learned and grown so much under your ministry. And Jerame, thanks for pushing me to write this book!

Dr. Stan DeKoven - Thank you for taking time to talk with me and counsel me. Your support has been immeasurably helpful and I'm very grateful.

Pastors Daniel & Theresa Jones - Thank you for always providing me with an amazing discipleship through the years. As I travel, I realize how blessed I am to be raised up under you guys. As you know, many of the stories in this book came from the ministry times at Summit.

Dr. Tal Klaus - Thank you for your help in proofreading and editing this book! I know you didn't mean to become the editor, but you did it so well I had to use your work. You and Dee have always been so supportive of my life over the years. Thank you!

To my family, intercessors, those who've financially supported my ministry, Johnson Doan, Summit Church, the Crux and DBC groups of times past, and friends all around, thank you for your constant encouragement and support over the years.

CONTENTS

FOREWORD

I am very excited about Andrew Hopkins' new book, *Carriers of the Ark*. This book is a must-read for all those who want to advance in the revelation knowledge of God in their lives. There is a huge difference between head knowledge and heart knowledge when it comes to knowing God. Many people know a lot of facts about God, but few actually know God.

Carriers of the Ark is a blueprint for those who want to carry the manifest presence of God in their lives and show forth the reality of Jesus as the King of Glory on the earth. I believe there is a generation like Jacob rising. This generation is comprised of individuals who will seek the face of God and change the atmosphere of schools, workplaces, churches, and families. This generation will be like that which we read about in the 24th Psalm of David: a generation that will be the ark of God, or the gates of heaven on the earth. This generation will live out and manifest Psalm 24:7-8, which says, "Lift up your heads, O gates, And be lifted up, O ancient doors, that the King of glory may come in! Who is the King of glory? The Lord strong and mighty, The Lord mighty in battle."

This Jacob generation will know their God and do great exploits. In fact, they will be like supernatural gateways that usher in the King of Glory through praise and a lifestyle of worship.

Let me ask you a question. Have you ever seen a gate lift up its head? The answer is no. Gates do not have heads, and gates do not lift their voices. The revelatory reality, which you will learn in Andrew's new book, is that we are the gates or arks that lift up their heads, and we are the voices of worship to the King. When we live out this role, we usher in the King of Glory onto the earth.

I believe that the journey you are about to take in reading this book will inspire you and launch you into the depths of God's love and into a greater intimacy with the King. I wholeheartedly recommend this book to anyone who wants to move past the outer courts of the normal Christian experience and into a realm of encounter with Jesus - that is where you become a carrier of the ark, His Presence, on the earth.

Jerame Nelson
Elisha Revolution
Author of *Burning Ones: Calling Forth A Generation of Dread Champions*, and *Manifesting God's Love Through Signs, Wonders, & Miracles*

FOREWORD

I first met Andrew Hopkins during the revival meetings we were holding in San Diego, 2016. A few weeks into the meetings, Andrew started handling the evening worship. Quickly, I saw he was an incredibly gifted worship leader, as well as a talented songwriter. His pursuit of the heart of God in his worship was compelling. It's been a joy to watch him release the sounds of revival in the earth.

I am excited that Andrew is publishing his first book, *Carriers of the Ark*. If you are to ascend to the next level and carry the glory of the Ark, this book is essential. It's a resource for training the future world changers.

This younger generation is passionate about revival and the supernatural. Many desire to have the demonstration of God's power flowing through their lives. However, they don't always have the pliability and perceptiveness formed by sacrifice and surrender. The passion is there but they need input and direction. *Carriers of the Ark* provides exactly what this generation is searching for. It will help them learn how to sustain the presence of God in their lives and future ministry. This book will reveal what God covets to form in us so that He can move through us.

There is much to discover and devour in this book. You will discover the unpopular keys to the anointing, the foundation of intimacy, keys to stirring up hunger, embracing the fire, and much more. In those moments of discovery, you will understand that discovery is not enough; you must activate and apply these truths in your life.

Do you want to be a part of the rising army of believers whose prayers are potent, whose worship moves the heart of God, and who speak with the thunder of God's voice? Then I recommend this book to you so you can be a carrier of the ark.

Joshua Mills
Bestselling author, *Moving in Glory Realms & Seeing Angels*
Palm Springs, CA
www.joshuamills.com

INTRODUCTION

In many ancient cultures, royalty was carried on what is called a palanquin or a litter. It was a chair or a bed, open or closed, carried by poles on the shoulders of servants. Carried by at least two to four, if not more servants, it called for physical strength to carry the royalty. The palki, as ancient India called it, was accompanied by singers, dancers, and storytellers[1]. You can imagine how the atmosphere would come under attention when a king showed up in one of these!

This vehicle of transportation is reminiscent of how the priests in the Old Testament would carry the Ark of the Covenant. The Ark carried the Presence of God. When King David brought the Ark successfully into Jerusalem, it was carried by poles on the shoulders of the priests while music and rejoicing were happening all around. David even took off his kingly robes in order to humble himself before the King of kings as God was welcomed in with honor to the center of Israel!

God wants to enter cities again with power and love, yet this time carried within the hearts of His people. When Jesus walked the earth, He was the glory of God clothed in human flesh. Now the hope of glory appearing on the earth is Christ in you. We are the modern day Carriers of the Ark.

All believers have the privilege to carry the King of kings into every area of life. We get to host His Presence wherever we go. Yet, just like the servants of old needed physical strength to carry the weight of the natural king, we need spiritual strength and inner fortitude to carry the weight of the King of glory.

This book is about what God wants to form *in us* so that we can carry more of Him *upon us*.

Many Christians want to have an external demonstration of God's power flowing in their lives yet don't always have the internal fortitude that's formed through surrender and sacrifice. Simply said, not everyone is willing to "pay the price." As a result, many have a hard time sustaining the flow of the anointing, the amount of "kingdom come" is limited, and even their own personal revival is capped. In other words, the world around us has limited gospel impact and people live underneath their God-given potential.

In this crucial hour for the church, God is raising up a generation who live fully surrendered to Jesus and have learned to keep in step with the Spirit. We were created to carry God's life-giving Presence and our world desperately needs it. I believe the reason you're holding this book is because you are one of these believers.

In the following pages, you'll receive teaching and impartation of qualities that make the everyday believer fit to carry and sustain the Presence of God on their lives. I've seen this stuff work firsthand and I believe God will use the content of this book to take you to a higher level. I'm praying that God moves powerfully in your life as you read. In Jesus name, amen!

Endnotes

1   https://artsandculture.google.com/exhibit/human-powered-sedans-the-sto-ry-of-palanquins%C2%A0-heritage-transport-museum/IAIy535Ha2n-Kw?hl=en

1

THE WAVE RETRACTED

"Posterity! You will never know how much it cost the present generation to preserve your freedom! I hope you will make a good use of it. If you do not, I shall repent in heaven, that I ever took half the pains to preserve it."
John Quincy Adams

Recently, I was reading a little booklet of a sermon transcription by Duncan Campbell entitled, "The Nature of a God-Sent Revival." It talks about the revival in the Hebrides Islands off the coast of Scotland that he was a part of. The publisher included a brief preface that had just as much punch as the rest of the book. In it the publisher writes:

> *"The cry of our day is, "Where is the Lord God of Elijah?" The question might better be asked, "Where are the Elijahs of the Lord God?""*[1]

God is looking for a whole generation of Elijahs (or better yet, Elishas) whom He can partner with to bring heaven on earth and establish His kingdom; people who are fit to carry the mantle of the double portion anointing.

When I read that statement I was gripped. I tried to keep reading the book but kept getting drawn back to that statement. As I meditated on that, because the Holy Spirit had illuminated it to me, the Lord showed me a vision.

I was standing on the beach where a wave had just gone back into the ocean. There was an older man to my left and a younger man in front of me. They were both standing on the shoreline and it was as if the younger man was waiting for the next wave. I knew it was about the waves of revival and the two people represented the older and the younger generation. The older generation had experienced a move of God.

I was a little frustrated, though. I was asking God, "Why did the wave have to go back into the ocean?" "Why can't the wave of revival just perpetually be here?" And God began to speak to me saying, "Because I'm forming *in* the next generation what *got* the older generation there."

I knew that God was alluding to the fact that the older generation paid a price to carry the anointing they had. The retracted wave gave the younger generation the opportunity to know what it is to be desperate for a move of God. When you watch the wave retract, or rather, hear the testimony of past moves of God, it develops within you a desire for it to return. In the midst of all that, it gives opportunity to develop humility, patience, hunger, passion, and purity while we wait. Each generation has to pay their own price.

When I speak of older and younger, I don't necessarily mean years, I mean maturity. That being said, many of the older saints (in age) paid a great price to see God move in their lives. They know what it is to travail in prayer, to fast and to pray, to study the Word, to believe God for miracles, to labor for souls and to see their families touched by God. Their worship is deep and moves the heart of God, their prayers are potent, and their words have the thunder of God's voice embedded within them.

Many of you reading this can think of some people like that at your church or in your life. They've walked through tragedy and triumph and still bless the Lord with all that is within them because Jesus has walked with them through it all. They know what it is to say to God, "I won't let go of You until You bless me." They're the kind of people who walk with "a limp" because they know what it is to wrestle with the Lord through the night season. They carry a seasoned joy and settledness about them that's compelling.

The question I ask is, if the older generation passes away, and the younger generation doesn't cultivate the inner fortitude of the former, what then will we be left with?

Who will continue to push the envelope?

Who will press on towards kingdom expansion?

Who will challenge the church to deeper depths and greater heights in God?

Who will provoke the people towards more?

Who will carry the ark on their shoulders?

Will we pass the mantle to a generation with anemic prayers, empty worship and impotent preaching?

Or will the next generation pay the price to carry the mantle passed on to them?

We are all called to be Carriers of the Ark of His Presence in our day. This entire book is about what I believe God wants to form in us in order to carry and host the weight of His glory. Instead of asking, "Where is the Lord God of Elijah?" let's become the next Elishas who are fit to walk in the anointing.

DO WHAT NO ONE ELSE IS DOING

I recently heard on a podcast interview[2] Evangelist Luis Palau tell a story of him and Billy Graham.

He recounts that they were hanging out in their hotel room with his assistant when they heard a knock at the door. The assistant went to the door and found a man there who was seeking to talk to Billy Graham for counsel. He said he was saved in one of Billy's crusades 20 years ago, wants to be an evangelist like Billy, went to seminary, has a team, has finances, but no invitations to preach!

The young man was invited in and they began to converse. Billy shared a few suggestions on what to do and time was up.

He asked Billy to bless him and so Billy led everyone in prayer. They all got on their knees and began to pray. After a few moments, Luis noticed that Billy's voice seemed to be muffled so he looked up.

What he saw marked him forever.

With tears heard in his voice, Luis recounted that when he looked he saw Billy Graham face down on the carpet of the hotel crying out to God for an evangelist he never met before and probably never saw again.

After they got up and everyone left, Luis remembers asking some kind of "dumb question" as he recalls it. And Billy responded by saying, "I read in 1 Peter 5 that if you humble yourself under the mighty hand of God then He will lift you up in due time. Theologians have their theories on that verse but I take it to heart."

After hearing that I was so moved by the humility and Christ-likeness demonstrated.

If we want to make an impact that nobody is making, we'll have to do things now that nobody is doing.

I'm sure we've all heard of the massive impact Billy made in the world for Jesus, but hidden behind the millions of decisions for Christ, the gospel preached to presidents and world leaders, and so much more, he had a life of uncommon devotion and passion for Jesus. Yet, even in light of all of the generals of the faith, like Billy and many others, we need an entire army of people whose lives are fully given to Christ and His mission.

James and John came to Jesus asking Him if they could sit on His right and left in glory (Mark 10:35-39). Jesus told them they didn't know what they were asking. He said essentially, are you able to pay the price for greatness? In other words, many people want the place of glory, but are we willing to pay the price in order to get there?

(For clarity, I'm not talking about trying to earn what we have by grace; I'm talking about a life of surrender and sacrifice in response to His grace).

D.L. Moody, another highly impactful evangelist was documented as having this encounter in the late 1800's:

"Henry Varley, a very intimate friend of Mr. Moody in the earlier days of his work, loved to tell how he once said to him: *"It remains to be seen what God will do with a man who gives himself up wholly unto Him."* When Mr. Henry Varley said that, Mr. Moody said to himself: *"Well, I will be that man.""*[3]

Will *you* be that man or woman?

Unpopular Keys to the Anointing

When the double portion anointing came on Elisha, it was he who made the declaration: "Where is the Lord God of Elijah?" (2 Kings 2:14). The anointing was activated, God showed up, the waters of the Jordan River split, and Elisha walked over on dry ground. But if we are to be the answer to the inverted question: Where are the Elijahs of the Lord God? (More specifically, Elishas), we would do well to go back a little bit before that and see what may have drawn God to choose Elisha to inherit the double.

"And so it was, when they had crossed over, that Elijah said to

Elisha, "Ask! What may I do for you, before I am taken away from you?" Elisha said, "Please let a double portion of your spirit be upon me." So he said, "You have asked a hard thing. Nevertheless, if you see me when I am taken from you, it shall be so for you; but if not, it shall not be so." (2 Kings 2:9-10)

I love how Elijah didn't sugar coat it. He said it's a hard thing. Many want a double portion of the anointing to fall on them, but are we willing to do what Elisha did to get it? I'm not saying we follow a cookie-cutter formula, but there are some characteristics in Elisha's life that would be good for us to follow if we are to be the people fit to carry the anointing.

When we first see Elisha in scripture he is plowing with twelve yoke of oxen (1 Kings 19:19-21). The guy who would eventually carry the infamous "double portion" anointing was a hard worker. In other words, God was looking for someone with a work ethic. Elisha wasn't sitting around feeling sorry for himself or waiting for God to do everything for him. He was found working. He was being faithful where he was planted. He was using what God had given him at that time. And God chose him to succeed Elijah. God is looking for people who are willing to work.

Elisha was also willing to surrender it all. He sacrificed his source of income! (1 Kings 19:21) He burnt it up. Now, there was no turning back. Talk about a cost. Halfway commitment produces halfway results. But Jesus said if you lose your life, you'll find it.

One of the keys to flowing in the anointing is surrender. You have to let go of your agenda, your ways, your plan - and surrender to His. It's trusting Him over yourself (Prov. 3:5-6). When God sees a surrendered heart, He says, "Here's someone I can work with." When you surrender in the little things, God sees someone who can be trusted in bigger things.

Elisha then became Elijah's servant (1 Kings 19:21, 2 Kings 3:11). Scholars believe Elisha served Elijah around 7-8 years. In a self-serving culture, this is an unpopular idea. To become the background guy, not getting any credit, not much attention…serving someone else's vision! And…dare I say it…*maybe not even get paid!*

This is a blow to our epidemic of selfishness. I thought God was all about me?! He is…in the sense that He wants you to become healthy like Him…and love isn't self-seeking (1 Cor. 13:5)

Do you know what happened in that 7-8 years? Elisha not only developed character and maturity, he learned the ways of the Spirit. Can you imagine being around the prophet who called fire down from heaven and commanded the rain? You're bound to grow in the Spirit.

I once heard John Thomas from Streams Ministries say, "You receive impartation from what you serve." He was sharing from his experience with John Paul Jackson and how he moved across the U.S. to come and serve his ministry. Through that, the anointing on John Paul's life began rubbing off on him - dreams, prophetic, seer anointing, and more.

Many people want the anointing to flow in their lives, but are they willing to go low and serve?

Elisha was and he got the double. (Side note: Elisha did double the amount of miracles that Elijah did. He was so anointed even his bones in the grave raised a dead man to life! (2 Kings 13:21))

When you're able to go low and serve it's a sign that you've become secure in who you are.

Elisha's life was marked by hard work, surrender and servanthood. Not to mention that Elijah tried to ditch him multiple times on his way out! It was Elisha's opportunity to develop hunger, tenacity, and heart that deals well with potential offense. This is what God wants to form in us as we seek Him and pursue the call to be Carriers of the Ark!

Sustain the Move

Pianos have a foot pedal called a "sustain pedal." It allows you to sustain the note(s) you're playing and gives a sound that makes the notes flow together. Without the sustain pedal, the notes are short-lived and choppy sounding. God wants our hearts to sustain the flow of the Spirit that He is releasing. He doesn't want the anointing to be short-lived and choppy. He wants the move of the Spirit to flow freely.

"And John bore witness, saying, "I saw the Spirit descending from heaven like a dove, and He remained upon Him." (John 1:32)

This is the life that Jesus lived. The Holy Spirit not only descended but remained upon Him. That's what we're after. Not a few moments here and there of glory, but the sustained Presence of God on our lives. This is something we learn as we grow in relationship with Holy Spirit.

The first time David tried to bring the Ark into Jerusalem, they did it in an uneducated way. They followed the way of the Philistines and used a cart driven by an ox. It was probably largely due to the fact that the Ark was neglected during the days of Saul's reign (1 Chron. 13:3). When the oxen stumbled, a man named Uzza took hold of the Ark and got struck dead for his error. It's a picture of when people don't know how to host the Presence, the flow of what God is doing gets quenched.

For example, when God wants to prophesy, but we end up teaching, we can quench the flow of what God is doing. Or vice versa. Jesus lived a life that kept in step with what His Father was doing (John 5:19). If we want to sustain the anointing in our lives, we need to stay in heart connection with the Father and do what He's doing.

David found out that the Lord had chosen the Levites to carry the Ark by poles on their shoulders (1 Chron. 15:1-15). This was the proper order or prescribed way. There was a right way to do it. Once they did it how God prescribed it, the joy and celebration returned.

"And the children of the Levites bore the ark of God on their shoulders, by its poles, as Moses had commanded according to the word of the Lord." (1 Chronicles 15:15)

When we're doing what God is doing, the flow of His Spirit is sustained.

POSITIONED FOR MORE

I can remember plenty of times when guest ministers would come and minister at our church in a more powerful way than I was used to. People shared their various strengths - prophetic, power, authority, praise and worship, and more. Each time that would happen, it was exposing me to more of the kingdom of God. It expanded my viewpoint and caused me to adjust my mindset so that I could make room for the new that God was exposing me to. Those encounters called me higher.

When God gives us encounters, they are meant to set the trajectory of our lives to go higher in God in at least two ways. One, it exposes us to more, which, when received properly, stirs us to pursue more. Two, everything changes and we have to adopt a new way to do things if we want to sustain what God gave us. (New wine doesn't work in old wineskins).

It's possible that, when God releases His power to a group of people, if they don't know how to sustain the Presence of God, before long, things will go back to "normal." The truth is, God wants to upgrade our normal! We want to be the kind of people who can sustain what God released and have the trajectory of our lives and ministry go higher in God.

We don't want to go back to "normal." God wants to consistently give us a new normal. Instead of treating encounters like a one time shock and then return to where we once were, encounters are meant to pull us higher. When we steward those moments well, with humble and hungry hearts, it serves to sustain what God has poured out and positions us for more.

Becoming this kind of person doesn't happen by accident. One of the ways you get the understanding and ability to sustain and flow with the anointing is by paying the price in the secret place with God (Matt. 6:6). It's where you learn to minister to the Lord, feel His pleasure and learn His heart. Time spent there will teach you how to keep in step with the Spirit and sustain His moving. It will teach you how to create an atmosphere of God's Presence - because you've learned what moves His heart.

Spending time in His glory allows you to be comfortable in His Presence. You will become familiar enough with Him so that you move when He moves. You sustain the anointing by staying where God is staying, going where He's going, saying what He's saying and doing what He's doing.

Sustaining His Presence is a dance and Jesus is the leader. People who can sustain the anointing do so because they're dancing with a friend whom they've come to know. They've learned the dance because they've spent time in the secret place with the Lord and found out what pleases Him (Eph. 5:10 NIV).

CARRY THE ARK!

When the Ark was successfully carried into the city, it was carried by multiple people. Pastor Jack Hayford says, "The Presence of God is borne by people, not things." It's not just a few individuals that God wants to raise up: it's a company of people.

These are people who not only have a love for souls, but they pray with potency, their worship moves the heart of God, and their words carry the thunder of God's voice! They've been captured by the mercy found at the Cross and responded by giving their all to Jesus. Rooted in Scripture, they move in the supernatural power of God with signs, wonders, healings and miracles.

These prophetic people have learned to walk in the Spirit and sustain the Presence of God through friendship with Him. We are a royal priesthood called to carry the Ark in our day! Christ in us and the Holy Spirit upon us!

We need entire churches that carry the Ark! Without the manifest Presence of God in our churches and lives, people can come and go and yet remain unchanged. No matter how good our music or preaching is or how many people we can gather in a room - nothing replaces the Presence of God.

It's time we pressed into a lifestyle that makes a landing place for the Lord to do whatever He wants to do. After all, He is the Lord!

OVERSIZED COAT JACKET

Years ago, I was in South Africa on a mission trip with my church. At one of the churches we ministered at, a man came up to me and handed me his coat. It was much larger than my normal size. The man said, "God told me to give this coat jacket to you as a sign that a bigger mantle is coming on your life. It doesn't fit you right now, but you'll grow into it." Looking back, I can say the anointing has increased drastically on my life since then.

I believe God wants to do the same for you! He is placing an oversized mantle on your life and calling you higher. You're called to carry the Ark of His Presence. It may feel like it's oversized, but you'll grow into it. Increased levels of encounters, intimacy, anointing and inner fortitude await you!

God is looking for not just one Elisha, He is looking for a whole generation of Elishas to carry the double portion anointing and the Ark of His Presence!

A Prayer to Get You There

Lord, I pray for those reading this right now. I pray a fresh anointing and an oversized mantle to fall on them now in the name of Jesus. Let the weighty glory of God come upon them in an increasing way. Take them deeper into Your Presence and teach them how to live in step with the Spirit. Be glorified in their lives in Jesus name. Amen.

Questions:

- Are there any older saints that you can think of who carry the Presence in a profound way? How has that impacted you?
- What do you think got them to the place they are with God?
- What costs has your journey been marked by?

Activations:

- If you have contact with an older saint, take time to ask them what their walk with the Lord has been like.
- Take time praying and singing in the Spirit. Let your relationship with Holy Spirit develop.
- Find a church or ministry to serve in. Find out what they need and help however you can.

Declarations:

- I will pursue knowing Jesus with all of my heart.
- I am growing in knowing how to keep in step with the Spirit and sustain the anointing.
- I honor the past generation's accomplishments by standing on their shoulders and going further.
- I lose my life for the sake of Jesus that I may gain it in Him.
- I am a carrier of God's Presence.

Endnotes

1   Duncan Campbell, The Nature of a God-Sent Revival (Vinton, VA: Christ Life Publications), p. 2

2   Nieuwhof, Carey, narrator. "The Carey Nieuwhof Leadership Podcast" CNLP 268, iTunes app, 3 June 2019.

3   https://www.eaec.org/faithhallfame/dlmoody.htm

2

THE FOUNDATION
OF INTIMACY

"It's not the people with oil who make it; it's the people with extra oil"
Charlie Robinson

There's a story of an old famous opera singer who would close all of his concerts with the classic song "The Lord's Prayer." Joined together with his beautifully trained voice, he brought an impressive performance. When he would sing it at the end of his concerts, the people would be captivated by his excellent voice.

One night, this opera singer visited a small church, where a young man sang the same song. At the end of the song, people got out of their seats and came forward without an official altar call. They began to pour their lives out to the Lord. At the end of the service, the opera singer went to introduce himself to the young man. The young man already knew who he was since his reputation preceded him.

The opera singer said to the young man, "I sing the same song you sang at the end of my concerts. But the people don't get moved like they do with you. I sing," he said, "and it's a religious song. But with you, and I don't mean any disrespect...you haven't had proper training. When I sing the song, I think they should be moved. Can you tell me why the people move with you and not with me?"

The young man replied, "You know the song, *I know the Man.*"[1]

God is looking for burning hearts who know Him deeply. They cry out with David saying, "One thing I ask from the Lord, this only do I seek: that I may dwell in the house of the Lord all the days of my life, to gaze on the beauty of the Lord and to seek him in his temple." They join those who sought the Lord outside the camp and linger longer in the Presence as Joshua did. They choose the one thing that is needed and sit at the feet of Jesus listening to every word He speaks. (Ps. 27:4 NIV, Ex. 33:7, 11, Luke 10:39, 42)

The original carriers of the ark were from the tribe of Levi, and the name Levi means "attached, or joined to." These burning hearts are those attached to the Lord in full devotion. David said it like this: "My soul clings to you; your right hand upholds me." Paul called himself a bondservant of Jesus. A bondservant in the Bible was one who was set free to do as they wished, yet out of love for their master, they chose to serve them for life. In other words, he willingly attached himself to the Lord for life. This is the generation of those who seek His face. (Deut. 10:8, Ps. 63:8 ESV, Ex. 21:5-6, Ps. 24:6)

Out of all the qualities I talk about in this book, this is the most important: intimacy with the Lord. It is the foundation to everything else. While it is not a means to an end, in that it brings fulfillment in itself, intimacy prepares you for destiny. Carriers of the Ark are those who've cultivated intimacy with God and have let that be the foundation upon which they build.

DON'T PUSH SNOOZE

I didn't grow up going to church. We had Christian "overtones" but I couldn't tell you much about Jesus or what it meant to follow

Him. I did, however, go to a Baptist pre-school where I remembered three specific things pertaining to God: David and Goliath, Noah's ark, and the idea that God saw everything. I remember my teacher saying that God saw everything and I pictured eyeballs everywhere around the classroom.

As a teenager, I was into skateboarding and partying. During that time, a few "alarms" went off in my life. Working at Taco Bell, a Baptist preacher came in telling me about the rapture, how he could be taken up and I would be left behind. He also told me I'd go to hell if I didn't have Jesus. That may not be popular preaching, but God was using him and he was loving in his approach. I was impacted and turned slightly towards God.

A week and a half later, I got into a car accident. I was going 70mph and slammed into the back of a Chevy Suburban while driving a 1983 Toyota Corolla hatchback. My friend in the passenger seat hit his head on the dash and had to get stitches. The friend seated behind me broke his nose on the back of my driver's seat, and the lap seatbelt went so deep into his stomach that it lacerated his liver. I somehow came out with only a few scratches and bruises.

We went to the hospital to have x-rays taken and I remember telling my sister, "I think God is trying to tell me something." And I told her what had happened at Taco Bell not too long before. It was like an alarm clock was going off in my heart.

Not too long after this, two of my best friends in my skateboarding crew wanted to commit suicide. We rescued one on a Friday night after he had been cutting his arm with a shaving razor, punching himself in the face, drinking whiskey and he took Vicodin. The next night, my other friend was threatening to drink a bottle of whiskey and drive his truck into a brick wall. He had gotten a new tattoo of his last name on his back and showed his mother that morning. She was so angry with him that she told him she hated him and wished he would've died when he was born. It all just shocked me.

It was like God kept sending alarms my way. You can only push the snooze button so many times before you miss your appointment. I was living a life I wasn't meant to live and He was calling me to Himself.

I started going to church with another good friend. In the process of a few months, God just wrecked me. I remember sitting in the back of youth group tearing up and not knowing why. People would pray for me and I would be a weeping mess. One particular time, visiting a small charismatic church, the preacher was preaching real good and I just started crying. I really couldn't control it. The woman sitting next to me just looked at me and said "that's the love of God." The Lord just kept drawing me.

The old way of life was getting shut down by all the tragedies and this new life was opening up. After sitting through many altar calls with my heart racing like crazy, I finally surrendered to Jesus at home. All I knew was that He made Himself real to me and I needed Him. Good thing everyone who calls on the name of the Lord will be saved!

RELATIONSHIP IS ROOTED IN ENCOUNTER

Everything that followed was an amazing journey of discovery. It was all new! I remember listening to the Word being preached on the radio and the life coming from the preacher's voice. There were many times of worship where the electric power of God would come or His peace would just rest upon me. The warmth of His Presence would come as I sought Him. I began to memorize scripture and study the Word. I didn't know anything so everything was new and intimacy with God began to develop. I spent a lot of time going after God.

I've often referred back to the countless times of worship in my car where God would come and dwell. I remember crying out that I'd rather be with God than anywhere else, the electric power of God was surging in my hands, tears flooding my face, all while I tried to make my exit off the freeway. Or declaring what Jesus accomplished for me on the cross and getting struck again by the mercy of Jesus, weeping on my way to work in my car.

Those times were the times I looked forward to in my day. They were consistent times of encounter. Relationship is rooted in encounter. This is how Apostle John put it:

"That which was from the beginning, which we have heard, which we have seen with our eyes, which we have looked at and our hands have touched—this we proclaim concerning the Word of life."

(1 John 1:1 NIV)

John essentially said, "We are preaching what we've had encounter with. I'm not telling you some clever ideas, theories, or philosophies. I'm proclaiming to you the One that I've encountered." He knew that if you only preach from your head, you'll only minister to the head. But if you want to reach the hearts of men, you have to preach from the heart. The heart is the place of encounter. Jesus isn't a lofty idea concocted by the minds of the religious scholars. He is a real Person and He wants to encounter you. Real relationship comes from encounter. Who can sustain a relationship with someone they never experience?

Many of us need a fresh encounter. As much as I loved what happened in the early years of seeking God, I need more. John the Apostle could've settled for what he had. He was the one who sat next to Jesus at the Last Supper and leaned upon His chest. Psalm 25:14 says, "The secret of the Lord is with those who fear Him, And He will show them His covenant." When John reclined upon Jesus, he was the one who got the secret of who would betray Him. (John 13:23-26) It was clear that John had a close relationship with Jesus.

Yet later on in his life, John was exiled to the Isle of Patmos. The one who could've settled in his intimate relationship with Jesus was awakened to more. He saw Jesus in a glorified state. There was a greater revelation of Jesus brought to him. The magnitude of Jesus was so great that John fell at His feet as though dead. Then Jesus began giving him prophetic messages for the churches (Rev. 1:10-20). It's time to seek Him until we find Him again! It's time for greater glory in our lives! There is more!

FUTURE SUCCESS STARTS NOW

David's testimony, before we knew anything else about him, was that he was a man after God's own heart (1 Sam. 13:14) and that he was a better man than King Saul (1 Sam. 15:28). Out of all the people in Israel that could've been chosen to be the next king, God zeroed in on a young man after His heart. Intimacy sets you up for destiny.

Even the prophet Samuel had no idea who the next king would be. He, along with David's father, thought it would've been one of David's older and burlier brothers. Yet the Lord spoke to Samuel and said, "Do not look at his appearance or at his physical stature, because I have refused him. For the Lord does not see as man sees; for man looks at the outward appearance, but the Lord looks at the heart." (1 Sam. 16:7). David was out in the fields taking care of his father's sheep and cultivating intimacy with the Lord.

Herein lies a powerful example. David wasn't seeking the Lord in order to become the next king of Israel. He wasn't doing it for status, promotion or the praise of man. He simply wanted God. He needed God. He wanted relationship. He wanted to know what was on God's heart, know His desires and please the Lord. Here's the question: if you want to be mightily used by God, how's your foundation? David's was solid in the Lord.

Cherish the hidden times. There's a difference between hiding and being hidden. Hiding has to do with shame but being hidden has to do with value and preparation. Adam and Eve hid because they were afraid and ashamed, but Moses was hidden because he was valuable. Hidden times are where God forms you for your destiny. David's mighty men of valor were formed in the Cave of Adullam where David led them in worship and taught them the fear of the Lord (Ps. 34). God will see to it that you are brought out of hiding at just the right time.

David was brought out of hiding when he defeated Goliath. When David went out, Saul tried to put his armor on him. David tried it out but he just wasn't used to it. You know what outfit David wore when he went out to defeat Goliath? His shepherd clothes. The very outfit he wore when he was found as a man after God's own heart and killed the lion and the bear. I like to call it his "secret place uniform." David's victory was grounded in his secret devotion to God.

It was like Ed Cole used to say, "Your private practice determines your public performance." We have an opportunity to dig deep wells with God through our time spent with Him. The revelation and encounters He shares with us become a deep well within. Psalm 141:3 says our mouths are doors, and just like Jesus (John 10:9) we are doors. Doors to what? To whatever fills our hearts. Whenever you open your mouth, you give voice to whatever is filling your heart. Fill yourself with God! So whatever you do gets the overflow of a rich relationship with Jesus!

GET YOUR OWN OIL

I remember one time being at an Intervarsity meeting on my college campus. A young man went up to sing and lead worship on his acoustic guitar. I was actually judging him in my heart because I wanted to be up there. I thought to myself, who is this guy and can he do what I can do? I was about to be graciously awakened. He started singing - with choppy guitar playing - and an accent that gave away the fact that English wasn't his first language. Yet the second he opened his mouth, the anointing of the Holy Spirit was upon him so strong I immediately teared up. Talk about swift repentance! This guy was obviously a friend of God. He had an oil reserve He was pulling from.

When prophet Samuel anointed David at the unction of the Lord, he literally poured oil on him. The Bible said that from that day on, the Spirit of the Lord came upon David in power. So much so, that when Saul was tormented by an evil spirit, David was called upon to play his harp, and under the anointing of the Holy Spirit the demon would flee and relief would come to Saul.

We need to store up for ourselves oil from the Lord - oil representing intimacy. In Matthew 25:1-13, Jesus tells a parable about five wise bridesmaids and five foolish bridesmaids. They all brought their lamps while they were waiting for the bridegroom to arrive. The wise ones, however, brought extra oil so they could keep their lamps burning. By the time the bridegroom showed up, the existing oil in all of their lamps ran out. The wise used their backup oil to refill with but the foolish had none! The foolish begged to have some of the wise ones oil, yet they refused them and told them to go and *buy oil for themselves*. This is a picture of what it looks like to either cultivate your own intimacy with the Lord or try to live off someone else's intimacy.

David's hidden times with the Lord caused him to have "backup oil" stored up in his heart. Note that in the parable they had to *buy the oil*. I believe this speaks of the cost of intimacy. It's taking the time to seek His face, surrender and minister to the Lord. David had already paid the price in the secret place of intimacy with the Lord. He had backup oil.

King Saul tried to live off David's oil. The baffling part about Saul was that he wasn't a stranger to the Presence of God. Earlier on in his life, he had a dynamic encounter with the Spirit of God where God gave him another heart and he prophesied with the prophets (1 Sam. 10:6, 9-11). So when David played the harp before him under the anointing and made the demon flee, he knew that Presence! What happened? He was living off of someone else's anointing and failed to surrender his heart to the Lord in repentance.

King Saul was like the five foolish virgins asking for oil in the midnight hour. When you lack intimacy with the Lord, you're the one that is left wanting in the time of need. It was said of Saul in 1 Chronicles 13:3 (NLT), "It is time to bring back the Ark of our God, for we neglected it during the reign of Saul." Saul had what I call a convenient relationship with the Lord. He only turned to Him when it was convenient. Backup oil is what makes you ready at any moment. You have a history with God that you can pull from.

This can happen in our day as well. We can try to live off someone else's oil, yet if we fail to surrender our hearts to the Lord and cultivate our own intimacy and anointing, we end up back in the same previous mess once they're gone. We can sit under anointed teaching, healing & miracle ministry, worship ministry, etc. but you can't take them home with you. The anointing on people's lives is meant to accomplish something in us, not make us dependent on them. Anointed ministry should provoke you to deeper levels with the Lord! I love learning from people who've cultivated something with the Lord; I just know that their relationship with the Lord isn't mine and I'm responsible to "get my own oil." It's like the old Ruffles Chips slogan, "Get Your Own Bag." It's time to "get your own oil"!

I love what Bill Johnson says regarding this: "It's impossible for me to impart to somebody my history with God. Every believer is required to make their own history with God. Where is history made? Primarily in the secret place."

When people don't have seasons in their life where they're willing to be a nobody and have Jesus be everything, it sets them up with a faulty foundation for the future. Whenever I see someone whose words and ministry carry the Presence, I recognize they paid a price in secret passion and hunger for the Lord to get that in their life. My respect goes up for the person and my heart opens up to the pure stream of the Lord flowing through someone who paid a price to carry what's on their life. Everything is birthed out of the secret place - revelation, ideas, strategies, songs, etc. There's an investment required in order to see the power manifest.

Your own intimacy causes you to have your own voice. You get first hand revelation from your time spent with the Lord. You're not just an echo of someone else because you've developed something in the secret place with the Lord. The frequency of Jesus begins to be found in your sound and atmosphere. It's not wrong to receive from others; they just can't take the place of your own relationship with the Lord.

> *"But you, when you pray, go into your room, and when you have shut your door, pray to your Father who is in the secret place; and your Father who sees in secret will reward you openly."* (Matthew 6:6)

WHY EXTRA OIL?

The extra oil not only brings massive fulfillment to the reason we're created, but it gives you ability to face life! Yes, it gives ability for ministry - anointing, gifts, leading people into encounter, etc. but it also equips you to have a godly response in whatever situation you face - relational challenges, parenting, finances, decisions, etc. You're pulling on a well of revelation from past time spent with God as well as a present relationship with Him.

Let me say this again in a different way: People lacking oil in the midnight hour are ill equipped for the demand at hand. They're out trying to get oil when they should've and could've been entering into a God-ordained moment. They're scattering in search for something they had opportunity to get in a past season. I love what Thomas Edison said:

"Opportunity is missed by most people because it is dressed in overalls and looks like work."

WE NEED THE WORD!

The first time David tried to bring the Ark into Jerusalem, the Lord struck a man dead for touching it. As mentioned earlier, it's a picture of when people don't know how to host the Presence, the flow of what God is doing gets quenched. Looking even closer, David said: "…the Lord our God broke out against us, because we did not consult Him about the proper order." (1 Chron. 15:13). The proper order was found in the scripture (Deut. 10:8-9).

People can get weird and unsafe when they don't know the Bible and don't adhere to what God has said. These guys were unaware of what the scripture said concerning what they were doing and they got judged for their error, or irreverence. If we want true intimacy with the Lord, we need to be people of the Word. The Word leads to encounters and encounters can lead us back to the Word. But if there's no Word to it, we shouldn't have any part of it.

Jesus told the Sadducees in His day: "You are in error because you do not know the Scriptures or the power of God"(Matt. 22:29). We need both the Scriptures and the power in order to stay in truth. Without either one there's massive imbalance. The atmosphere of power creates a heavenly way to view scripture. The truth of scripture provides accurate interpretation to an atmosphere of power.

It's time for a fresh hunger to be stirred in us for the Word. It's the most accessible gift we have to hear God speak to us. We've got so many free resources out there today like YouTube, social media, podcasts, Google, apps, etc. that have content that will assist us in our pursuit of God. But nothing compares to the Word. We've got to go to the source and get first hand revelation. It was Jesus' words from His own mouth that caused an increase in faith in Samaria (John 4:41-42).

During my first time preaching in Uganda, Africa, my friend and I were sent out to a bush church. I preached on the fire of God that should continually be burning in our hearts out of Leviticus 6. I had an altar call for salvation and one girl came forward. I barely touched her on the forehead and she went into a full blown demonic manifestation. As we were praying and commanding the demons to go, they started speaking back! This is what they said: "Stop it! Stop it! You're setting us on fire!" If they were trying to get us to stop that definitely wasn't the way to do it!

I found in Psalm 97:3 that fire goes before God and consumes His enemies on every side. I realized scripturally that the fire is there to not only burn in our hearts a passion for Jesus, but also to consume the enemies! The key to understanding was found in the Word.

God is looking for those who would burn with passion for His Word. Isaiah prophesied that God's attention is on those who tremble at His Word (Is. 66:2). Read, study and meditate on the Word.

CHRIST IS CENTRAL

On the road to Emmaus, Jesus appeared in a hidden form to two discouraged disciples. They talked with Him but didn't know it was Him. They were sad because they didn't understand the big picture of Jesus' death.

> *"Then He said to them, "O foolish ones, and slow of heart to believe in all that the prophets have spoken! Ought not the Christ to have suffered these things and to enter into His glory?" And beginning at Moses and all the Prophets, He expounded to them in all the Scriptures the things concerning Himself." (Luke 24:25-27)*

Jesus' answer to a discouraged heart was to teach the Word. More specifically, He taught the things concerning Himself! After their eyes were opened and they recognized Jesus, "...they said to one another, "Did not our heart burn within us while He talked with us on the road, and while He opened the Scriptures to us?"" (Luke 24:32)

It was the revealing of Jesus in Scripture that caused those disciples' hearts to burn! Romans 10:17 says that faith comes by hearing - and in many translations - hearing by the word of *Christ*. Faith comes by hearing about Christ. Christ is central. Jesus is the Author of our faith and the key to unlocking the understanding of Scripture.

If we want to burn in love and intimacy for the King, we need to meditate on the Person of Jesus in Scripture. True transformation comes from beholding Him (2 Cor. 3:18). The easiest way to behold Him is through meditating on Scripture.

POTENT PRAYER

A life saturated in Word and Spirit inevitably brings forth a potent prayer life. It's where you spend communing with the One you were created for with all kinds of prayers - conversation, intercession, declaration, petition, listening, and praying in the Spirit. Friendship is developed in the secret place. I learned how to pray by praying. My friend Taylor Jensen says, "Prayer isn't learned in a classroom, it's learned in a closet." You begin to see what He sees, feel what He feels, be moved by what He is moved by because your heart is connected to His. It's how David wasn't moved by the taunts of Goliath. He was living on a higher frequency than the fearful and disheartened people of Israel. His heart was connected to the One above the circumstances.

The Holy Spirit helps us immensely in this area. The gift of tongues is one of the most underrated gifts in the church. Every believer has access to this grace (Mark 16:17). I won't do an entire study on this here, but when you pray in tongues it is perfect intercession, you build yourself up, mysteries are unlocked, the devil doesn't understand, and you are able to commune with God on a deeper level. One of the most impactful people in church history, Apostle Paul, said he prayed in tongues more than the most charismatic church in his day! Praying in tongues is one of the most life giving things you can do, especially in regards to intimacy with God.

Not too long ago I was reading a sermon transcription from Duncan Campbell, a leader in the Hebrides Revival which began in 1949. He tells many amazing testimonies of how God moved, and one in particular struck me. He said he was preaching in a service in a part of the islands where the revival hadn't swept through yet. This place was hard and nothing seemed to be happening. He called for the praying men of Barvas (the city where the revival originally broke out) and particularly a young man named Donald. He eventually asked the young man to pray in the middle of his preaching.

"Now that morning at family worship they were reading Revelation 4 where John has the vision of the open door. "I saw a door opened in heaven." And as that young man stood, that vision came before him. And this is what he said in his prayers. "God, I seem to be gazing in through the open door. And I seem to see the Lamb standing in the midst of the Throne. He has the keys of death and of hell at his girdle."

Then he stopped and began to weep. And for a minute or so he wept and he wept. Oh, the brokenness. And when he was able to control himself, he lifted his eyes towards the heavens and he cried out, "God, there is power there—let it loose! Let it loose!"

And suddenly, the power of God fell upon the congregation...one side of the church threw their hands up like this. Threw their heads back and you would almost declare that they were in an epileptic fit, but they were not. Oh, I can't explain it. And the other side they slumped on top of each other.

But God, the Holy Ghost moved. Those who had their hands like this stayed that way for two hours. Now you try to remain like that with your hands up for a few minutes and you will find it hard-but you would break their hands before you could take them down. Now, I can't explain it-this is what happened."[2]

If that wasn't enough, while Donald was praying, the power of God swept through a village seven miles away and in every house someone got saved!

This entire revival was ignited because two elderly women decided to pray for the youth of their city and declared back to God what He said in Isaiah 44:3: "For I will pour water on him who is thirsty, And floods on the dry ground; I will pour My Spirit on your descendants, And My blessing on your offspring."

The place of prayer is the place of power. It's where people fall in love with Jesus and power is released into our world.

SONS OF THUNDER

Back when I was a youth pastor, we were at a youth camp and the Lord began speaking to me about the "sons of thunder." In Mark 3:17, Jesus gave the name "sons of thunder" to James and John. I had heard that they were named that because of their anger or outbursts - displayed when they wanted to call down fire from heaven on Samaria for rejecting Jesus (Luke 9:53). But that weekend it was like the Lord told me, "Do you really think I would nickname someone based on their weakness?"

Then I did a search and found that the thunder many times related to the voice of God in scripture. Look at Psalm 29:3 "The voice of the Lord *is* over the waters; The God of glory thunders; The Lord is over many waters." Or Job 37:2, 5: "Hear attentively the thunder of His voice, And the rumbling that comes from His mouth...God thunders marvelously with His voice; He does great things which we cannot comprehend." Even in Revelation chapter 4 there are thundering and voices proceeding from His throne.

When that young man prayed in the Hebrides Islands, the thunder of God's voice was found in his voice. There was power found in his voice. When Jesus named James and John the "sons of thunder" He was prophesying of their future - that not only were they born of the thunderous voice, they would carry the thunder of God's voice in their preaching.

God's voice carries a frequency that shakes down every structure in opposition to the gospel. The thunder of His voice can be found in yours through intimacy with the King.

In Conclusion

"And He went up on the mountain and called to Him those He Himself wanted. And they came to Him. Then He appointed twelve, ***that they might be with Him*** *and that He might send them out to preach, and to have power to heal sicknesses and to cast out demons"* (Mark 3:14-16, emphasis mine)

Before Jesus sent the twelve out to preach and do supernatural ministry, they were called to *be with Him*. This is the foundation of intimacy that we were created for. Carriers of the Ark carry a burning love for the King and prioritize being with Jesus.

Questions:

- What are some of your significant encounters with the Lord? How have they impacted your relationship with Him?
- How has God formed you in the hidden times?
- What makes potent prayers?
- What has been a key to intimacy with the Lord for you?

Activations:

- Take a week to meditate daily on a certain passage of scripture until inspiration comes.
- Make it a goal to pray in tongues a set amount of time every day for a week.
- Take time to wait on the Lord and ask Him if He has anything to say. Wait on an answer.

Declarations:

- I am part of a generation of those who seek God's face.
- I am being drawn deeper into intimacy with Jesus.
- God speaks to me and I hear His voice.
- Christ is central.
- I love reading, studying and meditating on the Word of God.

Endnotes

1   I first heard this from evangelist Harry Salem in 2006 and was deeply impacted.

2   http://www.revival-library.org/index.php/pensketches-menu/historical-revivals/the-hebrides-revival

3

THE KEY OF HUNGER

"One who is full loathes honey from the comb,
but to the hungry even what is bitter tastes sweet."
Proverbs 27:7 NIV

A few years ago, I was leading worship at a church overseas at a service they called "Hunger Night." It was my first time at this church and I didn't really know what to expect. Once I started leading worship, however, the hunger for Jesus in the room skyrocketed and we went places in the Spirit that I hadn't been to that often in corporate worship times. Their hunger put a demand on the anointing in a way that I wasn't used to. It pulled greatness out of me and called me higher as a worship leader.

Hunger pulls things out of heaven that don't come any other way. Hunger creates an atmosphere for God to move in. Take the Syro-Phonecian woman who wouldn't take no for an answer and even in the midst of a potentially offensive statement of Jesus, she pushed in for just the crumbs. Or the woman who had the issue of blood, who broke Levitical laws and pressed through a suffocating crowd just to touch the hem of Jesus' garment. Or Blind Bartimaeus (ex-blind) who didn't suppress his desperation for Jesus even though His main followers told him to quiet down.

I love what my friend Prophet Gary Zamora says about hunger: "Hungry people don't wait for an invitation…they don't wait for someone to agree with them." They just pursue Jesus! And God feeds hungry people (Ps. 107:9).

Carriers of the Ark are hungry people. They know it's the key to accessing more of God. Just as the Levites' portion and inheritance was the Lord Himself, these modern day Carriers of the Ark have become satisfied in Him and yet still hunger for even more.

GET IN TOUCH WITH YOUR NEED

One thing I know about hungry people is that they always find something to eat. I think it's hilarious when I do a fast that all of a sudden my body starts craving for food that I would never normally eat. I gotta shout "Get behind me Satan!" when that fast food commercial comes on TV. I even have to pray in panic tongues while driving by the local BBQ spot as the aroma of heaven makes its way to my air vents. The hunger is driving my flesh!

In the same way my flesh was crying out for food, when we recognize our need for Jesus, our hearts will cry out for Him! We discover and experience the reality that we don't live by bread alone, but by every word that proceeds out of the mouth of God! There's life found in Him that can't be found anywhere else. We find that He is the One who sustains and satisfies us.

We were created by Him and came from Him, therefore, our hearts are sustained by Him. In Jesus, all things are held together and He sustains all things by His powerful word (Col. 1:17, Heb. 1:3). We need Jesus - not only relationally, but we can't even make our heart beat without Him! Every breath we breathe is a gift from God. We are living because He *wants* us to.

Look at these desperate cries from the Psalms:

"My soul longs, yes, even faints for the courts of the Lord; My heart and my flesh cry out for the living God." (Psalm 84:2)

"As the deer pants for the water brooks, so pants my soul for You, O God. My soul thirsts for God, for the living God. When shall I come and appear before God?" (Psalm 42:1-2)

Then there's Psalm 63. The subtitle says: "A Psalm of David when he was in the wilderness of Judah." This is a potentially "dry" time for David. But this is what he said: "O God, You are my God; Early will I seek You; My flesh longs for You in a dry and thirsty land where there is no water." (Verse 1). Notice that he didn't say my flesh longs for water or food; he said it longs for God! There is no water yet his flesh was longing for God. We know he drank of the ever satisfying Presence of the Lord in times past, which provoked his present hunger, but David's longing arose from getting in touch with his deep need for God.

Later in the Psalm he said (verse 5 NIV): "I will be fully satisfied as with the richest of foods; with singing lips my mouth will praise you." Beholding and glorifying the Lord brought David a satisfaction to his heart that a first class meal would bring to his body.

Here's a verse you probably haven't thought all the way through before: "Then the blind and the lame came to Him in the temple, and He healed them." (Matt. 21:14) Think about that for a moment. People who couldn't see and other people who couldn't walk came to Jesus. My question is, how did they get to Him? Maybe the blind guys said to the lame guys, "Hey, my legs work and your eyes work. Let's get to

Jesus together - I'll walk and carry you, you just tell me where to go." Who knows?! The point is, their need for Jesus was greater than their inconvenience!

It's time to get in touch with our deep need for Jesus. This will stir hunger like never before.

FASTING & PRAYER

Jesus said, "Watch and pray, lest you enter into temptation. The spirit indeed is willing, but the flesh is weak." (Matt. 26:41). Jesus wanted His disciples to watch and pray but they kept falling asleep. He basically told them that their spirit wants to do the right thing but their flesh was holding them down. The Message Bible (MSG) translates the latter part of that verse like this: "There is a part of you that is eager, ready for anything in God. But there's another part that's as lazy as an old dog sleeping by the fire."

We all deal with the weakness of the flesh. One of the best ways to put our flesh in check is fasting and prayer. I was joking earlier about how my flesh starts crying out desperately for food when I go on a fast. What I'm doing when I fast is telling my body who's in charge. I'm telling my flesh that it will not rule me. Obviously, we need food to live, but fasting periodically puts our flesh in check. The voice of the flesh gets ruled by our spirit when we live a fasted lifestyle.

To be clear, it's not just fasting, it's fasting and prayer. Fasting dominates the flesh while praying builds you up. This will clear the spiritual "airwaves" around you and tune you into the things of God. Your spiritual sensitivity will heighten because you're intentionally seeking God all the while silencing the voice of the flesh and weakening its power in your life.

Jesus said, "This kind does not go out except by prayer and fasting." (Matt. 17:21, Mark 9:29). There are things in the spirit realm that just won't break until you fast and pray. I've seen much breakthrough in my life in prayer and fasting - from a deepening relationship with Jesus to breakthrough in finances and ministry help.

What does this have to do with hunger? It's not only a great way to dominate your flesh, fasting brings to the surface your innate desire for the Lord and His will. You're silencing the hunger of your flesh and amplifying the hunger of your spirit. Hungry people do whatever they can to get more of Jesus or the breakthrough they need.

Fasting is a lifestyle we're meant to live. Basically, Jesus said, "When you fast..." not "if you fast." (Matt. 6:16-18). This is part of the normal Christian life. Let me just add this: Fasting in scripture always has to do with abstaining from food to seek God. I know some people substitute fasting food by fasting social media, movies, etc. That's ok, but if you haven't fasted by abstaining from food, you need to try it out. The results are way too good to pass up. Also, take it easy when you're first starting.

Don't Pass Me By

"Pass me not, O gentle Savior, hear my humble cry; while on others thou art calling, do not pass me by." - Fanny Crosby

In the vision I shared in chapter 1, the wave was retracted and it was as if the younger generation was waiting for the next wave to come. I knew it represented the wave of revival. Like I said earlier, the retracted wave gave the younger generation the opportunity to know what it is to be desperate for a move of God and to develop hunger. It was their opportunity to develop a longing for a move of the Spirit.

I love the message of the finished work of the cross of Christ. There's a rest that we can enter into. But it doesn't diminish passion and hunger, it should actually stir more passion and hunger in us for not only what Christ has accomplished for us, but also what He's made available to us.

Someone could look at the hymn quoted above and say that it's not true to the New Covenant we have in Christ. But the reality is, Jesus is the Word made flesh to us. He is the revelation of the Father to us. There were multiple times in the Gospel accounts where Jesus acted as if He was going to pass people by in order to see what they would do. I believe God intentionally gives us these types of experiences in order to draw hunger out of us.

Jesus ignored Blind Bartimaeus when he first cried out. When Jesus walked on water, the Bible says He would've passed the disciples by. When He appeared in another form to the two disciples on the Road to Emmaus, He acted like He was going to keep walking when they came to the village the two were staying at. Jesus was drawing hunger out of them.

It may be that what you've interpreted as a "dry season" is really God calling a greater level of hunger out of you. You may have felt that God seems distant, but it may be that He is "passing by" in order to call you deeper. He wants to draw an initiative out of us. The good news is, if that's the case, there must be a greater realm He's inviting you into.

We can join the cry of ex-blind Bartimaeus and not let the nay sayers suppress our passion. We aren't going to let the Savior just pass by! I'm going to jump on what He's doing and draw as much life out of it as possible. The multiplication of the bread and fish didn't stop until the people had as much as they wanted. (John 6:11-12) In other words, their hunger determined the amount they got! Just like the supernatural flow of oil didn't stop until there wasn't any jars left to fill (2 Kings 4:6). As long as we're hungry, we'll keep getting fed!

TELL ME THE TESTIMONY!

When I first got saved, I was mentored by a couple that had been in the faith for years. They would consistently be teaching me the Word, showing me with their life what it meant to follow Christ, and telling me testimonies. I was so hungry to know what it meant to follow Jesus and I really didn't know much about anything so I soaked up whatever they told me.

There was one particular testimony that stirred my hunger the most. The man in the couple told me that he was invited to a Full Gospel Businessmen's Breakfast. There was a prophet there who ended up calling him out and telling him things about his life that he could only have known supernaturally. He was touched, but wanted even more. So every night he would kneel down by his bed and pray that God would make Himself real to him. He prayed this for 3 weeks. Unbeknownst to him, at the end of the 3 weeks, he had a dream where he was taken to heaven and was worshipping God. He woke up from the dream with his hands lifted saying out loud, "I praise You my God." He didn't know anything about the lifting of hands but apparently he learned in heaven!

That testimony stirred me to pray for God to meet me like He did for my mentor at the time. I prayed almost every night for more than 3 weeks. Around that time, there was a worship night coming to town with some well-known worship leaders. The preacher that night had an altar call, and I think it was for evangelism, not sure, but I just went forward anyway. As the worship team began to lead in worship, the power of God came on me like never before. My whole body was tingling with this power all over me. I got baptized in the Holy Spirit that night and it forever marked me.

After that I would just worship in my car to have that same feeling come on me. God would meet with me as I drove to work (as I mentioned earlier). The catalyst for that intimacy was having my own encounter with God and the catalyst for the encounter was the testimony! The testimony stirred a hunger in me for more!

Hungry people know there is more! They don't settle for where they are currently at in God. Testimonies make you aware of the more and tell you what is possible. From the testimonies in scripture to church history to modern day accounts, they are all revealing to us what is possible to enter in to. It was Jesus who said that we will do greater works than Him! (John 14:12). There's more!

Being in the Fire & Glory Outpouring in San Diego, we have an abundance of fathers and mothers in the faith coming in and telling the testimonies. Mahesh Chavda recently shared the miracle that his mentor Derek Prince considered the greatest miracle he ever witnessed. They were in a crusade in Pakistan, and there was a lady there with no eyes; she had nothing in her eye sockets. After they prayed and released the power of God, the lady came walking up to them and the Lord had given her two brand new eyes! They knew it was for sure her because they took a picture of her beforehand! Praise God!

There are so many testimonies to tell; from healing miracles, to financial breakthroughs, families being touched, inner healing of the heart, revivals throughout history, the gift of salvation and so much more! John said that if everything Jesus did were to be written down, the whole world could not contain the books that would be written (John 21:25). Not to mention the rest of history!

The point being, if you want to be stirred for more, feed on the testimony. Read the scriptures as testimonies, ask people what God has done in their lives, read books that tell the stories! When we hear what God has done, it's God letting us in on what is available to us.

EXPOSED TO MORE

Did you know it's possible to have church without Jesus? It happened in the Bible! Revelation 3:20 is a verse used many times for evangelism, but that's not the context. It says this: "Behold, I stand at the door and knock…" If Jesus is knocking at the door, that means He's not in the house! The church in Laodicea needed a wakeup call and Jesus was faithful to bring it. The point is, are you in an environment where Jesus is moving? We need environments that call us higher. One of the greatest ways to stir hunger is exposure. Get in a place where God is moving.

John Wimber is quoted with the famous saying, "The anointing is more caught than taught." You catch how to move with the momentum of the Spirit when you're constantly in environments where that is happening. Getting into a place where God is moving at a greater level than you're used to gives amazing opportunity to grow. In other words, it's hard to be satisfied with a 1983 Corolla hatchback when you got to ride in a brand new Tesla all day. You've been exposed to more!

Go to places where God is doing something different and more powerful than you're used to.

When I was a youth pastor, our kids worshipped on their knees and faces pretty consistently. It was always humorous when they invited a new kid to church and they experienced our worship culture. When our kids would go low, the new kid would look around and feel awkward being the only one left standing, so he would go ahead and bow with them. I love how the peer pressure was to go all out in worship to God!

The culture was set. If you wanted more of God, you just followed suit. It was a launching point for the kids to go deeper with the Lord... even if they didn't know they wanted it! The environment called them higher.

I purposely try to get around people who are farther than me in Christ so that I can go higher. And if I can't be around them in person, I'll read books, listen to podcasts, watch YouTube or check out their social media/websites. I want what they're carrying to rub off on me. After all, that's what the word anointing means: to rub off.

When I'm in an environment that the miraculous is constantly being demonstrated, my mind begins to get renewed to the supernatural being natural. My normal begins to shift. I go from thinking that miracles happen periodically to thinking they are normal to a believer's life.

As mentioned before, 1 Peter 4:10 says, "As each one has received a gift, minister it to one another, as good stewards of the manifold grace of God." When you're exposed to the grace on other people's lives, you receive of the many sided grace of God. You get something through them that you can't get anywhere else. It's the beauty of being a part of the body of Christ. Everyone has something unique to offer.

This is impartation; the sharing of spiritual gifts or a special grace or anointing on someone's life. Ultimately, impartation is from God, yet the uniqueness of the person God is using to impart makes a difference. I've received impartation from great men and women of God through the laying on of hands, being in their services, through dreams, books, and media.

I just get hungry for what God is doing in their life and how He is using them. God responds to that hunger (Heb. 11:6) and a measure of grace on their lives comes off on me. Sometimes, I see the gift at work in their life and I receive from just observing. Then there's an acceleration that happens in whatever anointing they imparted because now I don't have to start at square one. I get a supernatural boost that launches me into that anointing because I've seen how they operated and received the impartation.

It's time to get around powerful environments and people who are more hungry and anointed than you. Seek impartation. Proverbs 13:20 says: "He who walks with wise men will be wise, But the companion of fools will be destroyed." If you're walking with fools, people who've become stagnant in their relationship with God, it's time to find some people hungry for God and go deeper with Him! Compromise kills, but hungry hearts always draw closer to the King. I need to be around people who will call me higher!

HUNGER PULLS YOU

Hunger is magnetic. When you follow the God given hunger in your heart you'll end up where you need to be. Many of us wonder why we are pulled towards certain places and things but it's the Holy Ghost tracking system within you that locates your destiny and stirs your hunger for it. If you follow His leading, you'll end up in the right place at the right time.

I remember when I got saved people would warn me about the "false teachers." They talked negatively about them and it made me afraid of getting deceived. It's exactly what the religious spirit wants to do: have more faith in the devil's ability to deceive you than in God's power to keep you. The Holy Spirit is the Spirit of Truth! He will speak to you!

I began to do my own research on their teachings and found them to not only be scriptural, but also very powerful! The same Presence of God that would come in my personal worship times accompanied them. What's more is that they had more Biblical fruit in their lives than the ones who were trying to deter me! What does this have to do with hunger? I was called to walk in some of the things that the so -called "false teachers" were walking in, but my hunger was being blocked by a religious spirit.

I've studied to show myself approved unto God and have relationship with the Holy Spirit. Much of what I'm walking in today in the realm of the supernatural came from those who have controversy around them. Maybe a religious spirit is hindering your hunger. Maybe it's fear. Whatever it is, as we stay rooted in the Word and listen to the Holy Spirit, we will be led into our destiny. It's time to push past the hindrances and follow our God given hunger.

If I would've given up because of that religious spirit, I would've stunted my destiny. When ex-blind Bartimaeus cried out to God, the disciples told him to quiet down. But the desperation inside of him did not let the nay-sayers have the last word. He cried out all the more! We need a generation to tap into their God given hunger, push past the religious spirit and cry out for more! He got what he was looking for in Jesus. Hungry people don't stop until they find what they're looking for. His hunger set him up for his destiny.

Whatever God is stirring you up for you need to pursue it. He is drawing you to exactly what you need for the season you're in, as well as preparing you for your future - even if you don't understand it. The dryness you feel is God's way of causing thirst in your heart for the very thing you need. It's time to push in and seek God. I am in the midst of God's will for my life today because I followed the hunger He put in my heart. Years ago my hunger was drawing me to where I am now. The hunger that I now have is pulling me into where God has called me in the future.

The beautiful thing about hunger is that it never ends because there is always more. You experience God in an extraordinary way and may think that you've reached a high level in the Lord, but in reality, you've only scratched the surface. It's extraordinary to you because you've never been there before. But from everlasting to everlasting He is God! There's no end to the vastness of who He is! I love how Prophet Bobby Conner says, "We've become far too familiar with a God we barely know." That statement will forever provoke me for more.

HUNGRY PEOPLE ALWAYS GET MORE

God still satisfies the longing soul and fills the hungry with good things! Hungry people get on the fast track of spiritual growth because they aren't willing to settle. They don't compromise at halfway to their destiny or knowing God at the level they're currently at. They feel the pull to go higher and farther.

The greatest enemy of your hunger is complacency. Sometimes we need to stir ourselves up in the Lord (2 Tim. 1:6). Don't let the flame of your love grow cold. A.W. Tozer provokes us by saying, "The average Christian is so cold and so contented with His wretched condition that there is no vacuum of desire into which the blessed Spirit can rush in satisfying fullness."[1]

There's nothing that compares to Jesus. Deep down we all know it. Hunger boils down to the fact that we've tasted something that is beyond all this world can offer and we just want more. That's Jesus. Carriers of the Ark live with a core value of hunger because they know it's the key to accessing more.

Questions:

- How have you experienced your deep need for Jesus?
- What testimonies have stirred your hunger the most?
- What environments call you higher and deeper with God?

Activations:

- Search out testimonies of what God has done, especially in areas where you need breakthrough.
- Find a place where God is moving in a greater or different way than you're used to and attend a service/event there.
- Take time to fast and to pray, intentionally seeking to know the Lord more.

Declarations:

- I am growing in my understanding of my deep need for Jesus.
- I stir up my hunger for the Lord on a consistent basis.
- I pursue God with all of my heart.
- God is drawing me to my destiny.
- Regardless of how I feel, I continue to pursue more of Jesus in my life.
- I am hungry for the Lord and more of Him in my life.

Endnotes

1   A.W. Tozer, Tozer for the Christian Leader: A 365-Day Devotional (Chicago, IL: Moody Publishers) February 26

4

REPAIRING THE ALTAR

"Jesus paid it all, All to Him I owe;
Sin had left a crimson stain, He washed it white as snow."
Elvina M. Hall

I was in the Philippines not too long ago leading worship at a great church in Quezon City. I'm always excited when I get to lead there because the church is full of people who are hungry and passionate for God. At the end of the set, we sang about the God of the Breakthrough and I just felt that we needed to pray for people with metal in their bodies.

I called them forward and we began to pray. Within moments I heard shouts from the front and they brought a young man up to testify. He had been in a motorcycle accident where his skull had been crushed. Doctors placed a metal plate in his skull to help where the bone was broken. Through it all, the young man's right eye became blind. But in those few moments God restored his sight and the young man came up to show how he could now see! He covered his left eye and as I held up numbers with my hand, he followed me perfectly!

Another woman who was in a wheelchair also came forward. She didn't have metal in her body that I knew of, but apparently she had faith to be healed. I learned that she had a spinal injury that caused her to lose feeling in her legs and she couldn't walk anymore. Some people helped her up and began to walk her around the church. They brought her up to testify on the platform but I wanted to see her walk without help. They let go of her and I had her walk to me. She did it with no help! Jesus totally healed her!

God wants to break out in our worship services with miracles, healing, prophecy, intercession and a whole host of other kingdom things! True worship is a key component to having a supernatural atmosphere.

In 1 Kings 18, we find the infamous story of the prophet Elijah calling fire down from heaven. A great victory is won, God demonstrated His power, and the false prophets of Baal were executed. It was the demonstration of His power that was the turning point. However, there was one thing Elijah did that I believe is key: *he repaired the altar of the Lord.*

"Then Elijah said to all the people, "Come near to me." So all the people came near to him. And he repaired the altar of the Lord that was broken down." (1 Kings 18:30)

The altar represents worship and the word in Hebrew for "repaired" is "rapha." It's the same word where we get the name of God, Jehovah-Rapha which means, "The Lord Our Healer." When we see Elijah repairing the altar, it could also be translated that he *healed* the altar of the Lord. It's a picture of healing our worship unto the Lord.

If something needs healing, that means it's not functioning correctly, or not at its full potential. This is where I believe the worship of the church (in general) is: not at its full potential, and in some cases, completely broken down. There's so much more God wants to do in our worship times.

It was breakthrough praise that preceded God releasing those miracles in the Philippines. In Elijah's day, it was the repairing of the altar that led to the demonstration of God's power. If we want the fire to fall in our times of worship we must take the time to heal the altar.

This chapter focuses on what areas I believe need to be healed, or called to full potential, in regards to our praise and worship. Carriers of the Ark prioritize worshiping the Lord because they know that true worship is the key to sustaining the Presence of God.

The Frequency of a Broken Alabaster Jar

The reason the altar of the Lord was broken down in Elijah's day was because idolatry had been rampant in the people of God. I'll focus more on destroying idolatry in a later chapter, but for simplicity's sake, the key to breaking the power of idolatry is full surrender to Jesus. It's giving Him His rightful place in our lives as Lord. When Jesus is Lord in every area of your life, you reap the benefits of His Lordship in every area of your life.

God is looking for a sound that carries the frequency of a broken alabaster jar. It's the sound of sacrifice, the sound of surrender, the sound of a life laid down. That's the sound of worship. David said it like this: "…I will not sacrifice to the Lord my God burnt offerings that cost me nothing…" (2 Samuel 24:24 NIV).

A woman came to Jesus and poured out an extravagant offering on Him:

> *"While he was in Bethany, reclining at the table in the home of Simon the Leper, a woman came with an alabaster jar of very expensive perfume, made of pure nard. She broke the jar and poured the perfume on his head."* (Mark 14:3 NIV)

This offering she gave was costly, pure, and unreserved.

The disciples, with Judas probably taking the lead, complained and called it a waste. They said that it could be sold for more than three hundred denarii, which comes to almost a year's worth of wages (one denarius being a day's wages). That is a costly offering. It's costly to bring a gift that expensive. It's costly to give offerings into godly ministries. It's costly to worship God in the midst of pain. It's costly to worship through inconvenience. It's costly to consistently give of your time, talent and treasure. But nothing is ever wasted when it's poured out on Jesus. He's worth more than anything we could ever give Him. The reality is, all that we offer Him came from His hand in the first place; so we're really just giving Him back what already belonged to Him. It's a privilege.

The perfume was made of pure nard. In the Greek language, the word for pure means genuine and unadulterated. According to Thayer's Greek Lexicon, nard was often adulterated[1]. Adulterated by definition means "to debase or make impure by adding inferior materials or elements; use cheaper, inferior, or less desirable goods in the production of (any professedly genuine article)."[2]

If we want to repair the altar in our day, we need to purify our worship! We've added the inferior elements of complacency, irreverence, and boredom. We've become so concerned with what man thinks of us that we've lost the fear of the Lord. We end up watering down our worship and limiting the Holy Spirit because we're afraid of freaking out the new people. Our motives have been mixed with wanting to impress people and gain more "likes" on social media. We need pure hearts who've come in contact with their deep-seated need to know God. We need to rediscover the majesty of Christ and fix our eyes on Him.

Interesting to note, when Jesus cleared out the temple because they had turned His Father's house into a den of robbers, it was then that the blind and lame came to Him and were healed. Purity came to the temple and the miraculous broke out (Matt. 21:12-14).

This woman's worship was pure. She wasn't bringing watered-down worship. It was genuine and unadulterated; pure and fully devoted to Jesus.

It's also important to note that the fragrant oil was kept in the alabaster jar. According to Blue Letter Bible, the ancients considered alabaster to be the best material in which to preserve their ointments.[3] When she broke it open, she wasn't preserving it anymore. She was giving Jesus everything. She brought unreserved worship. In a room of naysayers, she poured out an extravagant offering. She finally found someone worthy to pour out her best offering on. It's the ultimate reason to worship: He is worthy.

The scripture says that as she did so, the fragrance of the perfume filled the house (John 12:3). The whole house was affected by her costly, pure and unadulterated worship. Just like the fragrance filled the house, let the frequency fill our sound - the frequency of a broken alabaster jar - that everywhere we'd go, our sound will call people to lay their lives down before the King in true worship.

IN VIEW OF MERCY

When I first got saved, all I knew was that Jesus made Himself real to me and that I needed Him. I couldn't tell you why He died on the cross; I had no understanding or revelation. One day I was reading Isaiah 53 after church and God opened my eyes. The line that God opened up to me was in verse 5: "the punishment that brought us peace was upon him." (NIV84). In an instant I knew that Jesus took my place when He died. I should've died there because the wages of sin is death, but He loved me and took my place.

I was undone with gratitude and my worship went to a new level. It was the mercy of God that captured me. I felt loved when I saw what He did. The power of God began to touch my life in a profound way as the gospel was opened up to me. I had a never ending source of fuel for my worship. The cross is the eternal declaration that we are loved by God (Rom. 5:8).

The part that amazes me is that He didn't *have to* - He *wanted to*. Apostle Paul wrote in Romans 12:1 NIV, "Therefore, I urge you, brothers and sisters, in view of God's mercy, to offer your bodies as a living sacrifice, holy and pleasing to God—this is your true and proper worship." He said the true and proper worship is in response to, or in view of, the mercy of God.

Why give your all in worship and surrender to Jesus? He is more than worthy and has paid the highest price for us. Matt Redman says, "Every authentic response in worship comes from revelation."[4] God opened my eyes to see the beauty of the Cross and it caused worship to rise out of my heart. I couldn't help but give Him worship.

I haven't even begun to scratch the surface of the worth and mercy of God, but my prayer is that God would give you revelation into His vast worth and incomprehensible love and mercy hidden in Christ. It's the source of eternity's worship. Take time to meditate on who the scripture proclaims Jesus to be. Ask God to open your eyes to the majesty of Christ.

EXPAND YOUR EXPRESSION

When I first started going to church, everything was new to me. I observed a lot just to find out what was normal. One thing that was weird to me, however, was when they sang a song about joy, the guy leading it looked bored! He said he was laying his sorrows down for the joy of the Lord but I wasn't so sure. In my head, the lyrics on the screen and the face of the worship leader did not line up. I didn't grow up in church, so maybe I missed something, but that was weird.

Plenty of years later, I understand there could've been all kinds of things that played into that moment. I could've just caught the worship leader when he was focusing on the chords he was playing. He could've just had a bad day. Who knows? But it made me think about expression in praise and worship.

Later on, my friends and I would go to big worship events with well-known worship leaders and the place would be electric. People would dance, lift their hands, shout, and just overall be passionate. We'd get back to Sunday church and it was like everyone turned into reserved and dignified people! The thing is, it was the same God we were worshiping in both places! He was still worthy of passionate praise!

One of the things we need to heal in regards to our worship is our expression. Since I didn't grow up going to church, I didn't have a denominational view of this. When I read the scripture, I found that expression was everywhere! It's even commanded! Sing, dance, shout, kneel, play music, lift your hands, etc. It's not a Pentecostal or charismatic thing, it's a biblical thing! And what's more, it's a human being thing!

I found that when you go to a comedy club or a movie, gut busting laughing is normal and accepted. When you go to a wedding, dancing is accepted. When you go to a sports game, shouting and lifting your hands is accepted. But when you cross the threshold into the church to magnify the Living God, the rules change and you're no longer allowed to be a human being anymore! Expression is tamed down and the fear of man is cranked up. Religion takes over and we don't let people express how they were created to.

I'm not talking about being out of order and disruptive. We've had times where people's expression was either inappropriate or distracting. In those cases we graciously ask them to stop. There's still an authority structure in order. I'm talking about the cases where people are both hindered from biblical expression or not taught and led into it.

One of the areas I find the hardest for congregations to enter into is the high praises (Ps. 149). This is the dance, the shout, and the passionate exuberance that God is worthy of. Even the Hebrew word "hallelujah" comes from "halal" which in summary means to act like a madman and be clamorously foolish! When we started bringing dance songs into our church, there were a token three people who would go with us. But I kept pushing it.

God was worthy and church shouldn't be boring! Not only would we do songs that talked about dancing before the Lord, I would share little nuggets from scripture to teach about the dance...and encourage people to start moving right then and there.

After some time, the place was a house of high praise. A lady in our church had gone into remission from cancer, so a bunch of friends were celebrating during the worship time. They broke into a conga line and danced around the sanctuary. It just happened to be a guy's first time visiting that Sunday! I asked him later what his first impression was and he said he thought we were crazy. But he also said there was something real there as well. He ended up staying and eventually became one of our church's worship leaders!

The scripture said it's the high praises that binds the enemy (Ps. 149). The high praises bring breakthrough to an atmosphere because it calls for passion from the people. In order to enter into passion you have to cross the threshold of passivity. You can't fully shout and dance passively! When the people of God begin to engage inwardly *and* outwardly, breakthrough occurs. Our outward expression *completes* our inward commitment to Christ. If you don't agree with me, just ask your spouse if saying "I love you" in your heart alone is enough.

If you do what you've always done you'll get what you've always got! It's time to expand your expression to God and in doing so, enhance your relationship with Him.

THE FEAR OF THE LORD

When David was bringing the Ark back into Jerusalem, it was carried on a cart led by oxen. When the oxen stumbled, a man named Uzza took hold of the Ark and got struck dead for his error (2 Sam. 6:7). The footnote in my NKJV Bible says the word for error is *irreverence*. Truly, irreverence is an error and it hinders the flow of the Spirit in our lives. It's the fear of the Lord that God wants to restore, not only to our worship, but to our entire lives as followers of Jesus.

There's a tension in the nature of God that we need to hold in balance. He is Abba Father and He is the All Consuming Fire. He is the One who stands in our defense and He is the Judge of all the earth. He is love and He is holy. He is the Lamb that was slain and Lion that has triumphed.

Paul asks us to consider both the goodness and the severity of God (Rom. 11:22). The same Jesus who blessed the little children also went into the temple, flipped tables upside down and drove people out with a whip. It's a New Testament statement that says it's a fearful thing to fall into the hands of the living God (Heb. 10:31).

Many of us are familiar with Psalm 34:8 that says, "Oh, taste and see that the Lord *is* good; Blessed *is* the man *who* trusts in Him!" Did you know that verse is surrounded by statements on the fear of the Lord? Verse 7 says that the angel of the Lord encamps around those who *fear Him* and verse 9 David sends out a cry, "Oh, *fear the Lord,* you His saints! There is no want to those who *fear Him.*" God's goodness is wrapped in the fear of the Lord.

To fear the Lord is to carry an honor, reverence, and preference for Him in every area of your life. It's a submission and humility before the King. To fear God is to consider Him in all your ways. His Word and Spirit become the filter through which you make your decisions. He reigns as King in your heart. This isn't out of a religious or legalistic approach, it's out of love and honor for the King. A.W. Tozer said, "No one who knows Him intimately can ever be flippant in His presence."[5]

It's still a sacred thing to stand in the presence of God.

If we want the atmosphere of heaven to come on earth, we should embrace the reverence of the throne room. It would be awkward for me to lay prostrate before a father, but, in the presence of a great King it would be completely appropriate. It's important for us to be struck with the massiveness of His being and be captivated by the unsearchableness of God.

"Oh, the depth of the riches both of the wisdom and knowledge of God! How unsearchable are His judgments and His ways past finding out! "For who has known the mind of the Lord? Or who has become His counselor?" "Or who has first given to Him and it shall be repaid to him?" For of Him and through Him and to Him are all things, to whom be glory forever. Amen." (Romans 11:33-36)

Matt Redman said, "When we face up to the glory of God, we soon find ourselves facedown in worship."[6]

WHERE'S THE SWORD OF THE LORD?

I was at a great church not too long ago attending the worship service. As a worship leader for over 17 years, I was not only enjoying the worship time, but I was also very aware of what was going on - musicianship, anointing, sound mix, congregation engagement, etc. It was all done very well and I was having a great experience in the Presence of God. But then the Lord spoke with His thunderous voice in my heart and said, "Where's the sword of the Lord?!"

It was one of the most intense times I've heard Him speak to me. I instantly started weeping under the anointing as the power of what He said rang throughout my being. I knew what He meant. He was looking for the prophetic edge to be released. He wanted to respond to the vertical worship that was being given to Him. Vertical worship is vital and necessary for the church to engage in, yet just like any healthy relationship, it's a two way street. God doesn't just want to receive, He wants to respond! This is how God designed worship.

1 Samuel 13:19, 22 tell us that the enemy had made weapons virtually non-existent in the army of Israel. The only ones with swords were King Saul and his son Jonathan. I believe it's a picture of what the enemy wants to do with the church today. He wants to make the church at large ill equipped for the battles at hand, leaving the swords only in the hands of a few selected leaders. I believe this speaks specifically to the gifts of the Spirit, and the sword represents the prophetic voice of the Lord (Heb. 4:12, Rev. 1:16).

The enemy wants to take the prophetic sword of the Lord out of our worship! He knows the power of God's voice. Yet now is the time for prophetic worship to rise across the body of Christ! If God has something to say, I want to hear it! This is one of the ways we repair the altar: we restore the prophetic to our worship times.

This may be easier to apply if you're in a worship or leadership position in ministry, but you can embrace the prophetic in your personal worship time as well! You can sing a new song and let God's voice speak through you and to you. Be on the lookout for worship ministries that embrace this and receive from the Lord through them.

This is how David's tabernacle functioned. It fully embraced the prophetic anointing in worship. In fact, it's how many of the Psalms were written. Take Psalm 46 for example. It starts out speaking about God:

"God is our refuge and strength, A very present help in trouble." (Psalm 46:1)

Then in verse 10 the narrative changes and God starts speaking:

"Be still, and know that I am God; I will be exalted among the nations, I will be exalted in the earth!" (Psalm 46:10)

This came out of one of their worship times! They had 24/7 worship going on non-stop with musicians and singers rotating through the day (1 Chron. 16:37, Neh. 12:24). The prophetic anointing came upon one of the sons of Korah and he starting singing the song of the Lord. Someone decided to write it down and now we have such a powerful promise to stand upon!

In other words, prophecy was a normal part of Israel's worship. There were 288 singers who were trained in songs of the Lord! I'm not saying that we are writing scripture with our prophetic songs, but I am pointing to the fact that the prophetic was normal in biblical worship. The question is, is it normal in our worship times?

I've ended up singing about the sermon that the pastor was about to preach on many occasions without knowing anything except following the leading of the Spirit. It serves to bring the awe of God into a room as well as a greater awareness of His Presence. Not only that, God's message was being broadcast in multiple avenues so as to bring supernatural emphasis.

You can access prophetic worship in at least 3 ways:

1. *Singing the songs that God is highlighting.* I love what Rick Pino says concerning prophetic worship: "Prophetic worship is singing the right thing at the right time." Singing through your song list can be genuinely prophetic when it's what God wants to say.

2. *Sing what you sense.* Many times I'll sing a scripture God is highlighting to me and it serves as a springboard into specifics He wants to say. It's doing and saying what you see the Father doing (John 5:19).

3. *Song of the Lord.* This is when God sings over His people and makes declarations to the atmosphere (See Zeph. 3:17, Ps. 44:4).

One time I was leading worship and flowing with my good friend Jerame Nelson at a revival service. As we flowed, I felt the Lord lead me to sing Malachi 4:2 that the Sun of Righteousness will rise with healing in His wings. Jerame then led into a time of releasing healing. A woman came up to testify that when I started singing that verse, she knew it was for her because the Lord gave her that verse that very morning. She testified to all the pain of glaucoma leaving her right eye! That's the power of the prophetic!

LET THE MUSICIANS PLAY!

It's not only what is being communicated in lyrics, it's what's being played by the musicians. David set up the musicians to prophesy upon their instruments (1 Chron. 25:1-5). The sound of the voice of the Lord can be heard without lyrics. The spirit of revelation can come upon a sound and the Lord can begin speaking to people without anyone singing. In the Garden of Eden, Adam and Eve heard the "sound" of the Lord God walking in the garden (Gen. 3:8). Even David was instructed to wait for the "sound" of marching on the tops of the Mulberry trees before advancing against the enemy (2 Sam. 5:24).

This is why many times I'll have the musicians do a "solo" or have the other musicians back off a little so one instrument can be highlighted. There's moments when the piano needs to lead, or the drums need to lead, etc. because the singer can't lead where God wants to go with their voice alone. There's something the musician's sound does that words can't. I'm convinced that the church/world is missing out on experiencing a measure of the grace of God because someone got religious and said we can't do "solos" in church because it brings attention to man.

"As each one has received a gift, minister it to one another, as good stewards of the manifold grace of God." (1 Peter 4:10)

People experience the grace of God *through people!* If we don't let the people use their gifts then we miss out on a measure of the grace of God. In other words, if the musicians can't play freely and even prophesy, then our worship is limited and we're not experiencing the fullness of what God wants to give us. This, of course, challenges our musicians to be competent on their instruments. There is so much prophetic potential within the sound of a worshiping musician.

When God speaks, supernatural power is released. Let's bring the sword of the Lord into our worship times!

VALUE THE ANOINTING

This calls for us to value the anointing. Prioritize the leading of the Spirit. It doesn't mean we throw out all planning and administration. We need both. Ezekiel's army needed both the bones and the breath to stand up on their feet (Ezekiel 37). It's the structure and the Spirit that work together.

When you value the anointing, you make space for Holy Spirit to move. If we want the sword of the Lord to come forth in our worship times, we have to make room - which means, at minimum, to make time for it. What if the breakthrough needed to take your church higher could be experienced by simply making time for Holy Spirit to move?

When God manifests His Presence, don't just rush through it because of a schedule. Bask in Him. Let God be God in your midst. Remember, it's Jesus who changes lives. Our work is empty and in vain unless God is in it (see Ps. 127:1). My good friend Charlie Fisher said that it wasn't until He gave God preeminence in His church services that He began to move in powerful ways - the manifest Presence of God filled the place, people didn't want to go home, worship leaders were raised up, the prophetic increased, miracles, signs and wonders, financial breakthrough, etc.

This doesn't mean *only* in the worship times. It's a worshipping heart that sustains the Presence of God. We can walk in that whether there's music or not. True worship is in spirit and truth.

Put Your Money Where Your Mouth Is

It was Jesus who said, "For where your treasure is, there your heart will be also"(Matt. 6:21). One of the keys to bringing full hearted worship to the Lord is using your finances. Praise God! I can feel your excitement. Jesus basically said your heart will follow your money. One thing I've always done is purchase worship albums. In doing that, I wanted to sow into my future as a worship minister, but also, my worship had more of my heart in it because *I paid money* to get those albums!

We'll spend $12 on a movie ticket and an untold amount on snacks at the theatre, but when it comes to worship music, we're looking for the free version somewhere on YouTube. Remember, wherever your money goes, your heart will follow. It's not bad to spend money on movies, etc, but if we never spend money on worship, our worship will be incomplete. This may sound self-serving because I have an album out, but the reality is I've been living this for almost 20 years, way before I had music out.

We also worship when we bring tithes and offerings. Deut. 16:16 says to not appear before the Lord empty handed. It's a blessing to honor God with the first fruits of our increase! (Prov. 3:9-10) It demonstrates whole hearted worship unto the Lord.

You may be familiar with the passage in Philippians 4:19, "And my God shall supply all your need according to His riches in glory by Christ Jesus." The context, however, is giving as an act of worship! Check out verses 17-18: "Not that I seek the gift, but I seek the fruit that abounds to your account. Indeed I have all and abound. I am full, having received from Epaphroditus the things *sent* from you, a sweet-smelling aroma, an acceptable sacrifice, well pleasing to God." Giving is one of the things that makes our worship complete!

True Worshipers

Jesus said that one of the things the Father is looking for is true worshippers who worship in Spirit and truth (John 4:23-24). He isn't looking for worship as much as He is looking for worshippers: people whose hearts are connected to His.

It was worship that transformed 400 men who were in distress, in debt, and discontented and turned them into who we know as David's mighty men (1 Sam. 22:2, Ps. 34). It was worship that caused the evil spirit to leave Saul as David played his harp. It was worship that caused the enemy to defeat themselves before Israel even swung a sword. It was worship that caused the prison to shake with an earthquake while chains fell off. And it's worship that is perpetually going on in heaven as the living creatures, elders and angels continually behold the beauty and majesty of Christ.

When David set up his tabernacle to house the Ark of the Covenant, he immediately appointed the praisers to minister before the Lord (1 Chron. 16). David knew the secret to invoke the pleasure of God - praise and worship. It was the key to sustaining His Presence. He learned it in the shepherd fields as a young boy where he was found as a man after God's own heart.

Let's take the time to repair the altar in our own lives and elevate our worship to a higher biblical standard.

"Great is the Lord, and greatly to be praised; And His greatness is unsearchable." (Psalm 145:3)

Questions:

- Has God spoken to you about any areas of your worship that need repairing?

- Where's your limit in outward expressions of praise? Are you willing to take it a step further?

- Have you ever seen the lack of the fear of the Lord? What about the flip side, where the fear of the Lord is present? Describe the difference.

- How have you been affected by the prophetic in worship times?

Activations:

- Ask God for a revelation of the Cross and what Jesus did for you.

- Ask God for a revelation of the worth of Jesus.

- Do a biblical expression of praise and worship that you've never done before.

- Buy a worship album!

Declarations:

- I praise and worship God with all of my heart.

- Jesus has forgiven me much, therefore I can love much.

- God sits enthroned on my praise. His kingdom power comes when I praise Him.

- I am growing in revelation of how worthy Jesus is.

- I will walk in the fear of the Lord.

Endnotes

1   https://www.blueletterbible.org/lang/lexicon/lexicon.
cfm?Strongs=G4101&t=KJV

2   https://www.dictionary.com/browse/adulterate

3   https://www.blueletterbible.org/lang/lexicon/lexicon.
cfm?Strongs=G211&t=KJV

4   https://www1.cbn.com/music/matt-redman%3A-living-out-a-%27heart-of-worship%27

5   A.W. Tozer, That Incredible Christian (Camp Hill, PA: Christian Publications, 1986), p.129

6   Matt Redman, Facedown (Ventura, CA: Regal Books, 2004), p. 13

5

REST & GLORY

"He makes me to lie down in green pastures;
He leads me beside the still waters."
Psalm 23:2

One time I was preaching at my church's young adult group on the topic of glory. I shared a story I heard about revivalist Smith Wigglesworth. When he would pray, the weighty glory of God would come so strong that people had to leave the room. It was too much for them to handle. A man heard of this happening and thought that if he ever had the chance to make it to one of those prayer meetings with Smith, then he would stay regardless of those who left.

The opportunity came and as soon as the man of God began to pray, the weighty glory fell, and the people began to leave. This is how the author recounts it:

"A Divine influence began to fill the place. The room became holy.
The power of God began to feel like a heavy weight. With set chin,
and a definite decision not to budge, the only other one now left in

the room hung on and hung on, until the pressure became too great, and he could stay no longer. With the flood gates of his soul pouring out a stream of tears, and with uncontrollable sobbing he had to get out or die; and a man who knew God as few do was left alone immersed in an atmosphere that few men could breathe in."[1]

I shared this story in closing and when I finished it, I closed my eyes and prayed, "Lord, do it in us Lord." As soon as I said that, I got hit with the power of God along with one other guy and ended up on the ground.

As the preacher, it can be a bit awkward when you're the guy laid out! I signaled to the worship team to play. It reminded me of when the priests could no longer do their work because the glory of the Lord filled the temple! (2 Chron. 5:14).

It was like God said to me, "How's that for "He makes me lie down"?"

It was this encounter that God began to teach me what it meant to rest in the Lord. I was seeking more of the glory, the manifest Presence of God. God was answering me by making me lie down and rest in Him.

If we're to carry a greater level of glory on our lives, we need to learn to rest.

SIT, WALK, STAND

I heard about this idea of "sit, walk, stand" from a friend but never looked into it. I figured this was a good time to seek it out. It comes from the book of Ephesians.

Ephesians 2:6 says that God "...raised us up together, and made us **sit** together in the heavenly places in Christ Jesus"

Ephesians 4:1 says, "I, therefore, the prisoner of the Lord, beseech you to **walk** worthy of the calling with which you were called"

Ephesians 6:11 says, "Put on the whole armor of God, that you may be able to **stand** against the wiles of the devil."

The progression is important. It started with sit, then walk, then stand. God was speaking to me about needing to sit first before walking worthy of my calling and standing against the enemy. The walking and the standing come *after* the sitting.

At this point, I had heard many teachings on walking out our calling and spiritual warfare, but I hadn't heard much about being seated in heavenly places. I didn't really understand what it meant. Why was it important for Christ to sit down at the right hand of God? What does that mean for me?

I had an NIV Student Bible from when I got saved, and one day as I was reading Hebrews 10, God opened my eyes…through a study note!

The passage was Hebrews 10:11-12 NIV84 which says: "Day after day every priest stands and performs his religious duties; again and again he offers the same sacrifices, which can never take away sins. But when this priest had offered for all time one sacrifice for sins, he sat down at the right hand of God."

The study note said this:

"Hebrews makes special mention that Christ "sat down" after finishing his priestly duties. Jewish priests never sat down; the tabernacle and the temple did not have seats. They did their work standing up as a symbol that it was never finished. Having finished the work of a priest once and for all, Christ "sat down.""²

Wow! The Old Testament priests never sat down because their work continued on and on and on, but Christ sat down because the work for our redemption was finished once and for all! When God raised us up together and made us sit together in Christ, He allowed us to freely enter into the finished work of Christ. Where Christ sat and rested, we also sit and rest in Him. We enter into *His rest.*

This is what's so amazing about grace - Jesus finished the work needed for our redemption, yet we get to enter into its benefits *freely*! Jesus did the work and we get the benefits! It's by grace through faith.

WHAT'S AT THE RIGHT HAND?

This opened up my eyes to see all that we have in being seated at the right hand of God. As we've already seen, it's a place of resting in what Christ has done for us, but God expanded on that and opened up more revelation on the specifics of that.

1. It's a place of receiving

Before Jesus released the miracle of the multiplication of food at the feeding of the 5,000, he commanded that all the people sit down. John's gospel explicitly says that they sat on green grass (John 6:10). Sounds a lot like lying down in green pastures!

Even on the Day of Pentecost when the Holy Spirit came upon the 120 disciples in the upper room, the Bible says they were all sitting! (Acts 2:2). The reference passage for all revival finds the disciples in a posture of sitting!

Sitting is a posture of rest, and it's in that position that God wants us to receive. It's a posture that says I trust You to do something for me that I can't do for myself. It's a posture that says I trust in God's grace and goodness towards me. He won't leave me like an orphan. He will come to me.

2. It's a place of closeness

Consider John who had a seat next to Jesus at the Last Supper (John 13:23). It was John who heard the secret of who was going to betray Christ. God releases secrets to His friends and we're in the right position for that to happen! (Ps. 25:14)

3. It's a place of joy & pleasure

Psalm 16:11 says, "…You will show me the path of life; In Your presence is fullness of joy; At Your right hand are pleasures forevermore."

Wow! Out of all the places God chose to put us, He put us in a place of pleasure and joy! And if it's God's kind of pleasure and joy, then you have to know it's the best in existence.

4. It's a place of heavenly perspective

Colossians 3:1-2 NIV says, "Since, then, you have been raised with Christ, set your hearts on things above, where Christ is, seated at the right hand of God. Set your minds on things above, not on earthly things."

We get to see life from heaven's perspective. Our hearts and minds see and think right when we're under the influence of God's glory realm.

5. It's a place of authority

Ephesians 1:21 says that the right hand of God is "far above all principality and power, might and dominion, and every name that is named, not only in this age, but also in that which is to come"!

Notice it's *far* above, not just a little above. We're seated in a place of authority far above every other power. God wants us there so we can rule and reign in Christ.

6. It's a place of fruitfulness

God brought me to the obscure story of when Joseph had Jacob, his father, bless his sons Manasseh and Ephraim (Gen. 48). Manasseh, being the firstborn, was on Jacob's right hand, and Ephraim on his left. But when Jacob went to bless them, he crossed his arms and put his right hand on Ephraim and left hand on Manasseh.

Yet, *Joseph knew the blessing was in the right hand!* So he tried to deter his father, but Jacob knew what he was doing. He was giving the firstborn blessing to Ephraim. I looked up what Ephraim's name means: "doubly fruitful"

God was sending the message that the blessing of the right hand results in fruitfulness. In other words, you bear more fruit for God when you live in the revelation of being seated in Christ's finished work.

What amazing benefits we get by being seated with Christ!

The Side Effects of Unfinished Work

Have you ever had a house full of unfinished things that need to get done? There's a sink full of dishes, the showerhead still isn't fixed, and the screen door keeps breaking off because the kids keep walking through it...

Or on a deeper level, trying to please a parent, pastor or boss, but nothing ever seems to work?

From small to big, the side effects of unfinished work can keep you in stress, worry or anxiety. If we haven't learned to cast our cares on the Lord and let it go, it can grow into feelings of shame or guilt, or striving, perfectionism, and getting too hard on ourselves. It can even affect us physically with sleeplessness or fatigue.

I remember there was a phase my wife and I were in that we watched every action/adventure movie out there - from Braveheart to Iron Man. There are always these intense fight scenes that caused me to tense up until the resolve came. Once the "bad guys" were defeated I could finally relax and breathe. I didn't realize how tense my stomach was during those intense scenes! I really appreciated the resolve that the victories brought because I could finally relax.

That's where we are in Christ; victory and resolve. God is for us. Period. We're fully accepted. We're fully forgiven. We're fully righteous. We're fully loved.

All of those side effects are flipped when we enter into the rest that God provided. We begin to truly walk in love - for ourselves and the people around us. We become ok with being a "work in progress" because we're not trying to prove anything. We've accepted the fact that we're accepted. We can sit and rest because all that was needed to obtain that was accomplished in Christ.

My friend and worship leader, Henry Haney, says, "Freedom is having nothing to prove and no one to impress." How is that possible? Because you know how the Father thinks about you and it has settled on the inside of you. Father God loves you with the same love that He loves Jesus with (John 17:23).

How Jesus lived His Life

Jesus is known as "the Son of His love" in Colossians 1:13. It's interesting to me that it doesn't say the "Son who loved" but the "Son *of* His love." He was known by how well He was loved.

At the waters of baptism, John baptized Jesus and the voice of the Father from an open heaven said, "This is My Beloved Son, in whom I am well pleased." (Matt. 3:16) This was before Jesus' ministry took place.

Again, on the Mount of Transfiguration, the glory cloud showed up and the Father spoke, "This is My beloved Son, in whom I am well pleased. Hear Him!" (Matt. 17:5). In John 3:35 & 5:20, the Bible speaks of the Father's love for Jesus, and in John 17:24 how He was loved before the foundation of the world!

In other words, Jesus lived from a place of resting in His Father's love and affection for Him. It was Jesus' food while fasting 40 days and nights (Matt. 3:16, 4:4). He lived off the words of His Father's love!

Jesus did more for the Kingdom in 3 1/2 years than most people do in 50+ years. Why is that? Because He was living from a place of rest. We're not seeking healings and miracles because we want a cool testimony to prove that we can do stuff; we do it out of the overflow of relationship with God and fulfilling His will. This is what we're created for (Eph. 2:10).

Jesus is inviting us to His way of life. There's a lot to that, but I know it means living a restful life as opposed to a stressful one.

Jesus said it like this:

"Come to me, all you who are weary and burdened, and I will give you rest. Take my yoke upon you and learn from me, for I am gentle and humble in heart, and you will find rest for your souls. For my yoke is easy and my burden is light."(Matthew 11:28-30)

If we want to be carriers of the Ark, this needs to settle within us.

HE TOLD ME NOT TO PRAY

Around this time, I was pastoring my church's young adult group and we were about to go on a retreat. I was about to go into my usual fasting and prayer time, as I would before the big events, and as I went to pray, it was dead and dry. There was no life in it. God spoke to me and said He didn't want me to pray for the event. I could hang out with Him but if I went to pray for the event the Lord would not be in it.

I wanted to be a good steward of the ministry He entrusted me with but if He said don't pray then I have to listen if I want His life to flow. When Jesus said to take His yoke upon us, it was representing what rabbis would do with their disciples. The yoke was a piece of wood that strapped the younger ox to the older one so it could train it to plow. It put a healthy restriction on the younger ox so it would keep in step with the leading of the older one. Jesus was "restricting" me so that I would learn His ways on how to "plow" or work properly. I was learning His ways of restful increase.

More fruit comes when we do it His way. That retreat ended up being one of the most fruitful retreats we had up until that point! God moved in such a powerful way with encounters for the young adults.

God was teaching me that rest and trust coincide. I was trusting my prayers more than the One I was praying to. It was me trying to walk worthy of my calling without having sat in Christ first. I had way too much confidence in myself; or rather, it was me performing for God instead of trusting that Christ's performance was enough.

Imagine that, just hanging out with God was more powerful than all of my praying and fasting from a place of performance.

One time I was about to pray at a service, and the Lord asked me in the middle of my prayer and said, "Why are you trying to take all the glory?" Again, I had such confidence that my prayer was going to move heaven, and people would look at me as some awesome man of prayer. He continued, "Just release My Presence and I'll do the work."

We should definitely pray in faith believing God will answer, but I was trying to prove that I could do it; that I was good enough. If I got approval, then I would feel enough…at least until the next time. It's a sick cycle that the "rest" of Christ breaks us out of. I was neglecting the opinion of God for my life. Truth is, I was already good enough and worth it to Him.

Galatians 5:4 NIV says, "You who are trying to be justified by the law have been alienated from Christ; you have fallen away from grace." In other words, when you're trying too hard in your own strength you have cut yourself off from Christ! You cut off the grace flow - the supernatural empowerment. Not a good place to be if you want to walk in the glory!

God wants to share His glory with us! (John 17:22) When Isaiah prophesied that God will not share His glory with another (Is. 42:8), He was talking about dead idols, not us. We come into that realm by grace. Not only does grace come to the humble, but grace causes humility - because we realize the greatness of the gift we have. We've done nothing to earn it and whatever we think we've done becomes irrelevant in comparison to the gift of entering into God's glory.

REST IS GOD'S IDEA

Through all of this, God was teaching me that He can do more in my rest than I can with all of my effort.

When I was preaching this stuff, some people got it misconstrued and took it as laziness. Just for clarity: the rest is internal. It's an internal rest that soaks in the love of God, spends time in intimacy with Him, and gets filled to overflowing with the truth of the gospel. It compels us to work the labor of love. We end up naturally living the way Jesus lived and end up being more productive - passion still intact!

From the very beginning, God even took a day of rest (Gen. 2:3). Did you know that Adam and Eve's first full day was a day of rest? They were created on the sixth day, God commissioned them to be fruitful and multiply, and their first full day on the job was a day of rest!

We work better when we work from a place of rest.

Yom Kippur, the Day of Atonement, was a day of rest (Lev. 23:32) because God wanted to send the message that the day that foreshadows your redemption is a day where He does all the work and your job is to believe and receive.

Many of Jesus' healings take place on the Sabbath rest day because He was showing them that when we rest, God works! (See also Ps. 127:2)

Jesus even said that Sabbath was actually *made for man*! (Mark 2:27)

What's the point?

Rest is God's idea!

ARM OF THE FLESH

One time I was leading worship and God showed me a vision of the arm of Jesus being crucified. He began to speak to me about the specifics of what that meant for me. Let me explain.

In 2 Chronicles 32, it tells the story of the king of Assyria coming against Judah and what king Hezekiah said to encourage his people: "With him *is* an arm of flesh; but with us *is* the Lord our God, to help us and to fight our battles." (2 Chron. 32:8)

The arm of the flesh speaks of what we can do in our own strength.

Later on Hebrews 10:20 tells us that Jesus made "…a new and living way which He consecrated for us, through the veil, that is, His flesh".

The veil is what kept people out of the Holy of Holies, where the glory dwelt. When Jesus was crucified, the veil was torn and God opened the way for us to enter into the glory.

But Hebrews says that the veil was Jesus' flesh. This sends a message to us about the flesh.

When the flesh was crucified, the veil was torn.

Jesus crucified the "arm of the flesh" in order to destroy our confidence in it.

Paul said it like this:

"For it is we who are the circumcision, we who serve God by his Spirit, who boast in Christ Jesus, and **who put no confidence in the flesh—"** (Philippians 3:3 NIV, emphasis mine)

"I have been crucified with Christ; it is no longer I who live, but Christ lives in me; and the life which I now live in the flesh I live by faith in the Son of God, who loved me and gave Himself for me." (Galatians 2:20)

Being crucified with Christ isn't saying "stop doing bad things and start doing good things." It's realizing our old sin nature died with Christ at the cross. It's walking away from the confidence we have in our old self and relying on Jesus' life in us; for Christ to live His righteous life through us. When Jesus said to "deny yourself" (Matt. 16:24) He was saying to deny your ability to do anything outside of Christ.

The entire context of Philippians 3 is not trusting in self-righteousness, but losing all for the sake of gaining Christ's righteousness and knowing Him. Jesus crucified His arm of flesh to prophesy to us that it's time for our confidence in our own strength to die.

Don't Trust the Veil

Just as the veil was hindering the people from entering into the glory of His Presence, our flesh does the same thing. Our flesh is the veil that hinders us from being in the glory. I always wondered why the veil was typified as Jesus flesh. Now I see that it was the destroying of confidence in ourselves and putting confidence in Christ.

Putting confidence in your flesh is like putting confidence in the veil!

This is why the phrase "self-made man" is the most contrary phrase to the gospel. It goes back to the Garden of Eden. The tree of the knowledge of good and evil was man getting knowledge that allows them to live apart from God. The most contrary message to the gospel is confidence in self outside of God.

So when Paul says he lost all for the sake of knowing Christ, he's saying I've lost all confidence in the things that have made me trust in myself and cultivate self-righteousness. Those things were huge enemies to the gospel and to Christ in him because Christ came to be his power source, not the works of performance for God.

Self-righteousness is working hard yet stuck in a box. No matter how hard you work, you're still stuck. You're still limited. It's like living in a warehouse with tons of resources yet there's no electricity so you can't see anything that you have.

So the new and living way was made through the tearing of the veil/the destroying of His flesh! The flesh was the thing hindering us from the glory! It was the veil! The more you're into the flesh, the more you're outside of the glory. But when the veil was removed and flesh was crucified, the glory was made available!

By destroying the flesh He was saying stop trusting in yourself and trust God. This releases the manifestation of His glory.

THE SMILE OF JESUS

Once I was praying and waiting on God in the beginning of the year and He showed me a vision of walking with Him in a field. I was following Him and when He turned around and looked at me, He smiled. Something about His smile and bright white teeth stood out to me.

As I meditated on it, I was reminded of how the Hebrew letters each have a pictograph meaning. The letter "shin" in ancient Hebrew looked like teeth and in some cases it meant to destroy, because your teeth crush food.

I knew Jesus was smiling to me not only to show His pleasure and love, but to destroy the mindsets of performance that had choked up the grace flow in my life.

I pray you see that same bright and pure smile of Jesus towards you today and that it releases you to go to new levels of glory. It's time to rest in what Christ has accomplished for you and be launched into the depths of His glory!

Questions:

- What does it mean to be seated with Christ and enter into His finished work?

- How does rest relate to walking in glory?

- Are there any areas in your heart that need to enter into rest?

Activations:

- Take some time to sit and wait on the Lord in prayer and worship. Ask Him how He sees you and how He feels about you.

- In a group: Have each person rotate sitting on a chair in the middle of the group. The group takes turns prophesying how God sees them and thinks about them.

- Take communion and thank God for all that Christ accomplished for you.

- Invite Holy Spirit to come and take you into a greater realm of glory.

Declarations:

- I am freely welcomed into and live in God's Presence at all times because of Jesus' finished work at the cross.

- I am continually drawn into God's Presence because of His great love for me.

- I consistently experience and receive the Father's love in my heart. My soul finds rest in His great love for me.

- I live from a place of rest in Christ, and work with a labor of love.

- Fruitfulness is increasing in my life because Christ is living through me.

- I put no confidence in my flesh. I trust God to move mightily in me and through me.

- I am consistently acclimating to greater measures and increases of the glory of God.

Endnotes

1   H.V. Roberts, New Zealand's Greatest Revival; Reprint of the 1922 Revival
Classic: Smith Wigglesworth (Dilsburg, PA: Rex Burgher Books [www.klifemin.
org], 1951), 46-47

2   Philip Yancey, Tim Stafford, NIV Student Bible, highlights in Hebrews
(Zondervan Publishing Company, 1996), p. 1283

6

EMBRACING THE FIRE

"But He knows the course I have traveled. *And I believe that* were He to prove me, I would come out *purer than* gold *from the fire*."
Job 23:10 VOICE

In December 2015, I wanted to quit ministry. There was tension in relationships, misunderstandings, and I just felt stuck where I was. The work I was doing for the past decade was great, but my issue really was: Would I ever get to do the things I had dreamed about years before? I had lost heart and I figured I'd just do something else. I halfheartedly wanted to go to culinary school and become a chef. I know they say, "Don't trust a skinny cook" but I really enjoy cooking! The problem with that was God wasn't leading me and I'm not moving if God's not moving.

I was stuck at a crossroads. I could compromise what I knew was the will of God for my life, or I could go through the fire. My wife and I knew that trusting God to make a way for us was far better than trying to make our own way.

This is where I believe the three Hebrew boys were at in Daniel Chapter 3. Long story short, their people had been exiled from Israel and relocated to Babylon where King Nebuchadnezzar ruled. The king had made a huge image of gold and commanded that everyone worship it at the sound of the music. If they didn't, they'd be thrown into a fiery furnace. These boys, known as Shadrach, Meshach, and Abed-Nego, could either compromise their commitment to the Lord and end up ineffective or go through the fire.

The three Hebrew boys resolved that they would not compromise their worship to the Lord and as a result got thrown into the fire. The scripture said that the boys were thrown in *bound* and fell down in the fire. Yet in a startling change of events, the king stood up in astonishment and saw not three, but four men *loose* and walking in the midst of the fire! Jesus came in their midst! And the Bible said they came out with no harm from the fire! Not only is that a wild supernatural miracle, but here's what I want you to see: *the only thing that burned off them was the thing binding them.*

This is why we need the fire of God! God wants to set us free from the things binding us; the things holding us back in life. The Bible tells us that after they came out of the fire, the king literally *promoted them* and exalted God.

Carriers of the Ark are people who embrace the fire of purification. Many people want the promotion but don't want to face the fire. It's one of the ways God burns off the things that bind us and releases promotion in our lives. People who carry glory understand that strong character is just as important as gifting. If you embrace the fire, you'll see the promotion!

WOE IS ME!

Years into ministry, I started feeling sorry for myself. I was disappointed that I never had a worship leader mentor. I had leaders still speak into my life regarding worship, but never had a worship leader take me under his wing and mentor me. I learned a lot by trial and error, copying other worship leaders, searching online resources, reading books, and really just worshiping God on my own. But I felt inadequate; like I was missing something. Maybe I was missing some secret principle that everyone else knows…lol.

It caused me to get unhealthily introspective and function out of a victim mentality. I was saying "woe is me" internally and blaming everyone else for my insecurity. The "if only" syndrome started making its way into my thinking: "If only I had a mentor…", "If only someone would've helped me", "If only I went another route", then everything would be better. I realized that God allowed me to go through the fire to burn off this mindset and insecurity because it was holding me back.

One of the things God wants to burn off His people is a victim mentality. It's a mentality that puts us in a position of acting powerless over our current circumstances. We may not be able to control what happens to us, but we are always in control of how we respond. I had the responsibility to use whatever I had at the time to give my best offering to the Lord in worship leading. I had to do something with what I had instead of complaining over what I didn't have. As I did, God was faithful to bring exactly what I needed to grow me in my calling.

It's interesting to me that when Jesus healed the man at the pool of Bethesda He asked Him if he wanted to be made well (John 5:6). Or when Jesus healed the blind man He asked him what he wanted (Mark 10:51). Jesus was giving them the opportunity to take initiative. It's the first step out of the victim mentality.

Did you know that Jesus doesn't want to control you?

That may be a shock for some, but it's the truth. Lordship doesn't mean controlling. Controlling has to do with insecurity - and Jesus is definitely secure in who He is. The famed French General, Napoleon Bonaparte was quoted as saying it like this: "Alexander, Caesar,

Charlemagne, and myself founded empires; but what foundation did we rest the creations of our genius? Upon force. Jesus Christ founded an empire upon love; and at this hour millions of men would die for Him."[1] People will willingly give their lives not because of force, or a controlling spirit, but because of love.

He gave us the Holy Spirit and one of the fruit of the Spirit is self-control (Gal. 5:22-23). Jesus wants us to manage ourselves well and He gave us a supernatural ability to do it. But He doesn't want to control you. That's your responsibility. That's why we can't blame others for our actions; it's always our choice.

This is freedom! And responsibility. This cuts at the heart of a victim mentality because now you can't blame anyone anymore. You get to forgive based on the forgiveness God has given you in Christ and move forward into your destiny. (For more on this, check out Danny Silk's book entitled "Keep Your Love On").

It's time to take charge of your life and move into freedom! God expects you to do something with what you have! Don't bury it in the sand (Matt. 25:25).

EMBRACE SONSHIP

I was serving at a women's Christmas dinner banquet at my church years ago (the men served the ladies), and they had a prophetic minister speaking. At the end of the night, the leaders had the guys come up who were serving to receive ministry. This lady prophesied to me pretty much everything I'm doing today as a traveling minister. She even told me I wouldn't be at the church too much longer. Back then I was elated that I got the word and confirmation. After all, I had been dreaming of traveling for years.

I went back to the sound booth where I was serving, and got on my face in gratitude before the Lord. I saw a picture of my pastor in my head and the Lord said, "Remember your father." I knew I was to receive the confirmation and stay faithful where I was serving my spiritual father. I said yes in my spirit and kept on doing what I had before me.

Romans 8:29 says, "For whom He foreknew, He also predestined to be conformed to the image of His Son, that He might be the firstborn among many brethren."

Out of all the titles Paul could've used here for Jesus, he used Son. He could've said "the image of His Christ" or "His Prophet" or "His Teacher." Yet, He specifically used the title: Son. This is important for us because that is the unique identity that God is forming us into. There's much more to be said than we have space for here about what being a son entails: Father's love, joy, freedom, peace, etc.

God was calling me to walk in sonship. The spirit of sonship (see Rom. 8:15) is ultimately between you and God, but it plays out in your heart attitude, especially towards leaders in your life. When we enter into sonship, God begins to burn out the orphan mindsets in us.

The questions for me were: Could I serve someone else's vision faithfully? Could I submit to their leadership in my life? Could I lay down my selfishness and follow through with another's wishes? Could I remain loyal to another man's ministry all the while having dreams of my own ministry burning in my heart? Could I be a faithful son to my pastor?

We would do this for Father God as His children, yet it plays out in being faithful right where we're currently at.

Thankfully my pastors are loving and gracious and allowed me much freedom to pursue the gifts and calling on my life. They did untold amounts of things that set me up for success in gifting and character. Yet, even in all of that, my heart still needed purification from the orphan spirit.

The orphan mindsets retort with thoughts like: "They're just using you for your gift", "You are more gifted than the pastor, you should start your own church", "You need to get out there and make a name for yourself", "They're just about their own thing, you need to fight for yourself!" The orphan mindset is all about itself, selfishly hoarding, ungrateful and resists servanthood because of insecurity. It needs man's approval for survival. Sonship lives from the Father's love freely given to us in Christ; it's a security rooted in Father's love.

But remember, although the spirit of sonship plays out in how we relate to our leaders, it is ultimately between you and God. Through this season of being purified by the fire, God never said to go anywhere else. I was right where He wanted me and I trusted Him enough to open a door when it was time. Sometimes we want to run as fast as we can away from these scenarios, but God knows what He's doing and we can trust Him. We just need to listen to His voice.

Just to clarify, I'm not talking about being a doormat to be walked all over or to be in a spiritually abusive relationship. We need healthy boundaries in our lives. But sometimes what we perceive as unsafe or hurtful is actually the Father using people in our lives to purify us of mindsets that are holding us back. If we run away from every confrontation, we could miss the opportunity for breakthrough and healing in our lives. On the other hand, we need to be firm on healthy boundaries in order to protect what's most valuable to us.

I knew it was important for me to serve as a son in the house and be faithful where I was planted.

STAY FAITHFUL WHERE YOU'RE PLANTED

"Those who are planted in the house of the Lord

Shall flourish in the courts of our God." (Psalm 92:13)

In order to flourish we need to be planted! This is one of the ways the spirit of sonship is developed in you and the orphan mindset is burned off. We are planted in the church. (1 Tim. 3:15 actually says the house of God is the church). We need fathers and mothers to speak into us, we need brothers and sisters to relate to, and we need sons and daughters to pour into.

Throughout my years serving as the worship leader of my church, I had many opportunities to go elsewhere and take other jobs. But I knew that God had placed me where I was and until He opened the door, I wasn't going to move. I chose to be faithful where God had planted me. Just like a tree needs to be planted in order to grow, we need to sink our roots into the local church if we want to flourish. And stay until God says! It's healthy for you and the people you minister to.

One day I was reading Psalm 68 and it opens like this: "Let God arise, Let His enemies be scattered." It's reminiscent of what Moses would say when Israel was moving through the desert. The cloud would lift, the people would pack up, and as the Ark moved forward, Moses would say the same thing (Num. 10:35).

As I kept reading Psalm 68, I found this verse:

"God sets the lonely in families, he leads out the prisoners with singing; but the rebellious live in a sun-scorched land." (Psalm 68:6 NIV)

Remember, the context of the Psalm is reminiscent of when Israel would travel through the desert with the cloud covering them by day. Everyone had a tribe - hence, God set the lonely in families. But if you decided you didn't want to be a part of the congregation, then you would be what the verse calls the rebellious who "live in a sun-scorched land." The Hebrew word for "families" there is the same word translated "house" in Ps. 92:13 from earlier.

It's a picture of what happens when you decide that having a godly community isn't for you. Not only is it called rebellion, but you live in a "sun-scorched land" where it's dry and lifeless. The rebellious removed themselves from the supernatural cloud covering in a scorching Middle Eastern desert! Simply put, when you take a hot coal from the midst of a burning fire and set it aside, it will end up cold and ineffective.

On the other hand, planted people flourish. They are activated, anointed, transformed and equipped to live like Christ! Church is not the *end all* place; it's the *send all* place! It's training ground for world changers. It just doesn't always look like the way we expected it to. You may have wanted it to be the launching point of your worldwide ministry after serving one year, but God wanted it to be the place of humility and servanthood.

NO COMPROMISE

One of the things I love about the story of the three Hebrew boys was their unwillingness to compromise. It was a lifestyle they committed to even before the fiery furnace incident. No matter what came their way, they were sold out to the Lord.

God is looking for a people who will stand on truth regardless of what culture is saying and doing; to walk in holiness, purity, and righteousness according to the scripture. If you're bowing when everyone else is bowing, you won't stand out. These boys literally stood out of the crowd and when they got through the fire, their stand made a national impact for the Lord. We can either compromise and be ineffective or we can go through the fire and not only see God glorified, but also get the promotion!

One of the areas that people are tempted to compromise in is media; music, movies, TV, social media and the like. One day, within the first year of following Jesus, I got out of church singing "God of Wonders" and then on my drive home had music playing that glorified a one night stand. I felt convicted because of the contradiction in my mouth. One moment I'm blessing God, the next moment I'm singing of immorality.

Something had to change. I got rid of a lot of music. I didn't want to feed my flesh.

It's crazy to me how Christians will pay money to watch blatantly demonic movies then wonder why their faith is weak and they're getting attacked spiritually. Our eyes and ears are gates through which we allow things to enter our lives. It's important to keep guard over what we watch and listen to. Our belief systems are formed by what we hear.

I'm not saying we become overly religious, throw darts at Santa and only watch TBN or Daystar. A great question to ask is what spirit is dominating my environment? Who is reigning in my house? Bottom line, we want lives of purity that honor Jesus.

PROMOTION COMES FROM THE LORD

"Then the king promoted Shadrach, Meshach, and Abed-Nego in the province of Babylon." (Daniel 3:30)

Like I said earlier, I wanted to quit ministry. Although the Hebrew boys didn't get harmed by the fire, it didn't say they couldn't feel it. It's like the southern mamas say, "If you can't stand the heat then get out' the kitchen!" I almost got out' the kitchen but I'm so glad I stayed.

A month later at the end of January 2016, Jerame & Miranda Nelson hosted a prophetic conference in San Diego. Our church had begun to connect with their ministry so we planned on attending. What started as a four day conference never ended. It turned into what is called the Fire & Glory Outpouring and has been going for over 900 nights by the time of this writing. Many miracles, signs and wonders broke out, salvations, breakthrough, and so much more. The King showed up and released His glory.

Our church partnered with the outpouring and our worship team led much of the worship times. I began to travel with Jerame to release the fires of revival all around. At this time I was still on staff at my church as Worship & Young Adult pastor as well as serving two nights a week in the revival. Our first son was also seven months old at the time. Needless to say, I was a busy man!

By the end of 2016, my wife and I had a meeting with our pastors and the Nelsons. The topic was to transition me off the church staff and to work with the Nelsons and start my itinerant ministry! Wow, to think that I was considering quitting when the door to my breakthrough was just a month away! And it was the very thing I had dreamed of - revival and traveling ministry! Talk about a promotion.

"For exaltation comes neither from the east nor from the west nor from the south. But God is the Judge: He puts down one, and exalts another." (Psalm 75:6-7)

There's no way I could've made that happen. Promotion comes from the Lord! It's so much better when God does it. Don't try to make your destiny happen on your own. Trust God. Be faithful. If you humble yourself before God, He will lift you up in due time.

In Conclusion

Our first son recently learned how to ride a bicycle. A whole new world opened up to him as it's totally different without training wheels. He wants to go down big hills now but I get so nervous because he hasn't fallen enough to know how to handle bigger things! Many people want to just automatically get elevated into huge things in ministry but they haven't gone through many trials and don't have the fortitude that trials give us (see Rom. 5:3-4, James 1:2-4). Your proper response to your trial wins for you a voice that moves mountains.

The path to your destiny is paved with fire. In other words, you're gonna go through some tests, some stretching, and some pruning on the journey to your destiny. God's will in the midst of it all is to purify your life - to get rid of the things that are holding you back - and set you up for promotion. In my life, God was dealing with selfishness, pride, entitlement and some orphan mindsets. But I'm so grateful for the fire.

I want to encourage you to stick it out, stay faithful, trust the Lord. Just like Israel, if the cloud doesn't move, you shouldn't move either (Num. 9:17-18). God has you where you are for a reason. Soak up all the nutrients from this season so you are well equipped for the upgrade in the next season.

Carriers of the Ark have an inner fortitude that is formed in the fire. Remember, God is for you!

Questions:

- Are you being faithful where God has planted you?
- What is God burning out of your life?
- Are you aware of Jesus Presence with you in the fire?

Activations:

- Ask a leader in your life if there's anything they see that needs adjustment.
- If you're not already serving, find a place to serve in a ministry context.
- Write a thank you note to someone in leadership in your life for how they've impacted you in a positive way.

Declarations:

- Jesus is with me in the fire. I am not alone and never forsaken.
- If God is for me, who can be against me!
- God is forming me to be like Jesus, a Beloved Son.
- I can do all things through Christ who strengthens me.
- I walk in the spirit of sonship and honor those above me, beside me and beneath me.
- I will be faithful where God has planted me. As I am faithful with little, God will entrust me with much.
- I will flourish as I am planted in the house of the Lord.
- I trust God with my future.

Endnotes
1   https://www.goodreads.com/quotes/111826-alexander-caesar-charlemagne-and-i-have-founded-empires-but-on

7

KILLING IDOLS

"You have made us for Yourself, O Lord,
and our hearts are restless until they rest in You."
Saint Augustine

About a year after I got saved, Chris Tomlin came out with a worship song called "Enough." The words of the chorus say:

"All of You is more than enough for all of me

For every thirst and every need

You satisfy me with Your love

And all I have in You is more than enough"[1]

This was my anthem to the Lord. It was everything I wanted and needed to say to Him. The album had this song and "Here I am to Worship" back to back and I would use these songs to express my heart to the Lord daily. Especially as a young man, there were so many things competing for the affections of my heart. This song kept me in the realization that nothing can satisfy me like Jesus.

Colossians 1:16 says that we were created by Jesus and for Jesus. The Message Bible says, "...everything got started in him and finds its purpose in him." The invention needs to go back to the Inventor in order to know what it was invented for. The creation needs to go back to the Creator in order to know what it was created for. We will never find our true purpose in anything else other than Jesus because we were made by and for Him.

I used to liken it to my old 1983 Volvo 240DL. If I took that thing off-roading, it would probably start breaking down because it wasn't made for that. In the same way, when we put our lives in the hands of things or people, we will start falling apart because we weren't made for them, we were made for Jesus!

One day, as I was driving to my community college, I was stopped at a traffic light. The song "Enough" was playing in my car and the reality of the lyrics hit me again. "All of You is more than enough for all of me."[2] I asked myself, do I really believe that? I prayed a prayer that day that had a massive impact in my life. I said, "Lord, if she (referring to a future wife) never comes and I never get to fulfill the dreams in my heart, I promise You that You will always be more than enough for me."

I suppose another way to put it is, "Lord, I'm committed to rid myself of idols all the days of my life and keep You first, for You alone can satisfy." As the years have passed, the Lord has given me both an amazing and beautiful wife as well as open doors to go after my dreams. Yet, at the end of the day, He alone can fully satisfy the longing in my heart.

Colossians 1:18 says, "And He is the head of the body, the church, who is the beginning, the firstborn from the dead, *that in all things He may have the preeminence*" (emphasis mine). Preeminence literally means to have the highest place or to be first. In other words, all creation is designed to work properly when the Lord is in first place. When other things fill His place in our lives, we get the result of a lesser lord ruling our lives: fear, hiding, lust, greed, independence, and the like.

The Lord is looking for people who would put Him first in all things and find ultimate satisfaction in Him. It's actually the healthiest place to be. God wants it for us because He loves us and wants the best for us. It's what we were designed for and it's the order in which God created everything.

Carriers of the Ark know that nothing satisfies like the Presence of God! They've settled on the inside that Jesus is more than enough for them.

IDOLS FALL IN THE PRESENCE OF GOD

In 1 Samuel 5, the Ark of the Covenant was captured by the Philistines and taken into the house of their god, Dagon. They placed the Ark next to their god. The next day, the people came back early in the morning and the Bible says this: "...there was Dagon, fallen on its face to the earth before the ark of the LORD. So they took Dagon and set it in its place again." (1 Sam. 5:3).

Now, if you have to help your god, he's probably not god. That's your first and only required sign that you need a new god. Just needed to say that.

The next day, the same thing happens, yet this time the head and the hands were broken off! Imagine that! God is wreaking havoc in the enemy's camp without anyone's help. The Lord isn't intimidated at all. In fact, He is dominating in darkness.

The Lord begins to break out against the enemy with tumors (some translations say hemorrhoids) and many died. His Presence destroys the enemy and his works. It's a picture of what the Presence of God does in our lives. The Philistines realized they needed to get rid of the Ark if they wanted to survive. They sent it to two other cities and eventually back to Israel. When glory breaks out, the enemy does not like to be around.

Here's what I want you to see: The idol had no choice but to fall in the Presence of Almighty God. It's the antidote to idolatry in our lives: Taste and see that the Lord is good! God will begin to tear down idols in our lives as we enter into His Presence. Some may think we need to get rid of the idols in order to enter in, but the truth is, just get those idols near the Almighty One who satisfies and they lose their power.

GOD-SIZED EXPECTATIONS

Fast forward a couple thousand years and Jesus is sitting at a well with a woman having a conversation. He tells her that if she drinks of the water He gives, she'd never thirst again. As she basically says yes to Jesus for His water, He asks her to call her husband. The truth comes out that she has had five husbands and the one she is with now isn't her husband. That's six men, if you're counting. She shifts the conversation to worship and Jesus basically tells her He is the Messiah, the One she had been waiting for. He became the seventh Man.

When Jesus said she'd never thirst again (John 4:13), He was saying she'd never thirst for another Source again. When you're drinking the living water He gives, You know He's more than enough. He completed the emptiness in her heart. He could do for her what the other six men couldn't. She finally found what she was looking for in the person of Jesus.

One of the things God wants to deal with in our lives is putting God-sized expectations on people. As much as this is stating the obvious, it should still be said: people are not God so we shouldn't expect them to be.

Jeremiah said it like this:

"For My people have committed two evils:

They have forsaken Me, the fountain of living waters,

And hewn themselves cisterns—broken cisterns that can hold no water."

(Jeremiah 2:13)

I remember one time when I was youth pastor, one of the youth guys came up to me all distraught. I had just shared in the message about how in heaven there's no marriage (Matt. 22:30). He wanted to make sure he heard me correctly! He was apparently so in love with his girlfriend at the time he couldn't fathom the thought of heaven without being married to her! It was a tough one for him.

One of the people we can put way too many expectations on is our husband or wife! (For the single people, your future spouse!) We act like once we have a mate, all of our troubles will disappear. That doesn't even work in our relationship with Jesus!

I'm not proposing to write a manual on marriage here, but what I do know, is that if you expect perfection from your spouse, you set yourself up for disappointment and put way too much pressure on them to perform. Lighten up, have fun and realize there's only one God. Your spouse or future spouse is not God, so to expect them to give you what God alone can give you is unhealthy and ultimately, idolatry.

"You open your hand and satisfy the desire of every living thing."
(Psalm 145:16)

Psalm 16:11 also says that there are eternal pleasures at the right hand of God - which is where you are seated in Christ! In other words, the ultimate satisfaction is found in the Person of Jesus, and you are placed exactly where He is.

Pursue intimacy with God and your spouse (or future spouse) will thank you. Also, you will bring more to ministry than a gift. There will be an atmosphere that follows you. Working from a place of intimacy plugs you into a source of life that never runs dry. Intimacy trumps principles every time.

People Are People

I remember, years ago, doing a sound check one time when I was leading worship for a mid week service at my church. Apparently we didn't sound as good as I was hoping because the next pause we had in between songs a guy spoke up and said, "It sounds like a garage band in here." Then as we continued to rehearse another lady held her hands over her ears and mouthed to me, "It's too loud!" Now, I bet other worship leaders could tell me way worse stories, but we hadn't even gotten to the service and I was already discouraged. I was already caring too much what they thought, but if I was getting my source from them, I'd be completely sunk!

I love what Bill Johnson says concerning this: "If you don't live by the praises of men you won't die by their criticisms."

People are people. We're all under construction and definitely not perfect. Fathers, mothers, siblings, leaders, bosses, and friends all fall under the category of "imperfect." This is why it's not a good idea to draw your life from the opinions of people. The same people who shout your praises one day may be the same who sharply criticize you the next day.

What God Thinks of You

Nehemiah 8:10 provides us with the famous passage that says, "The joy of the Lord is your strength." I was meditating on that one day and I saw it in a new light. It's the joy of the Lord, not of us. What makes God joyful? Besides the fact that He's inherently joyful because He is God, I know that He rejoices over us! (see Zeph. 3:17). When God thinks about me, He gets happy! And when I know that, it makes me strong!

Let's take this a little bit further. Psalm 139:17-18 tells us that God's thoughts about us outnumber the grains of sand. Jeremiah 29:11

tells us that the kind of thoughts God is thinking about us are thoughts of peace and not of evil. The Hebrew word for "peace" is *shalom*. Shalom is basically every good thing you ever wanted in life: peace, health, total well-being, prosperity, contentment, wholeness. Ephesians 1:4 tells us that God chose us before the foundation of the world and John 17:23-24 tells us that God loved us before the foundation of the world with the same love that He has for Jesus.

God has been thinking of you.

How long? *Since before time began!*

How much? *More than could ever be numbered.*

What kind of thoughts? *The very best!*

What did He do with those thoughts? *He chose you! And loved you with the same love He loves Jesus with!*

Think about that.[3]

Jesus is the Beloved Son in whom God is well pleased. In the Greek, the word for "beloved" can mean "favorite." It's easy to say that Jesus is the favorite, but to realize that the Father loves me the same way He loves Jesus is incredible! God preferred us, cared for us, thought us worthy of love and made the ultimate sacrifice for us on the cross!

FAITH IS ACTIVATED BY LOVE

There's a story in Scripture of a man who was paralyzed and was brought to Jesus by his friends (see Luke 5:17-26). The first thing that Jesus said to the man wasn't "be healed" or "get up and walk." It was actually, "Man, your sins are forgiven." One of the greatest ways we experience God's love is to experience His forgiveness. I want to encourage you if you feel paralyzed in your sins, your past, your fears, or whatever is holding you down - Jesus is saying the same to you. "Your sins are forgiven." God isn't counting your sins against you because He already counted them against Jesus at the cross. All you have to do is accept it.

The Bible says that faith works by love (Galatians 5:6). In other words, faith is energized and activated by God's affection for us. Jesus knew this man's faith needed to be activated. In that day, disease was often viewed as a sign of God's judgment. This man probably thought God was punishing him, if not for the potentially incriminating fact that he just interrupted the meeting by his friends breaking through the roof! He needed to know he wasn't in trouble! Jesus came to clarify God's heart for him and firstly released love and forgiveness. That love energized and activated his faith so that when Jesus told him to get up and walk he could respond in faith and do it. God's love cleared away the cloud of unbelief and activated faith in this man. Let Him do the same for you today.

When the love of God begins to fill your heart, it brings a transformation of self. He begins to heal wounds, take away shame and drive away fear. One way you can know the love of God is transforming your life is that you gain a healthy view of yourself and at the same time you take your eyes off yourself. The love of God brings value to your view of self yet at the same time makes you selfless.

Apostle Paul wrote that love "does not seek its own" or "is not selfish" (1 Cor. 13:5 NKJV, NIV).

Sometimes we can get overly religious about that verse and deny ourselves to the point that we don't value ourselves. But that's not healthy, it's not what Jesus came to give us, nor is it how He lived His life. Jesus lived with confidence in His Father's love and at the same time was completely selfless. That's what the love of God does for you.

God's love fills your tank so much so that you're not looking to others to fill it, you're actually looking for others to pour into. In other words, you're not an empty or half full cup looking to be filled, you're an overflowing cup looking to give away what Father has given you! Confidence comes because you know you're loved and selflessness comes because you know you're already taken care of in that love. David said it like this in Psalm 23:5 "...my cup overflows." This, my friends, is a process of transformation.

God's love brings security to our hearts. There's a restfulness that comes in knowing who you are and how much you are loved. On the other hand, insecurity drives you to be so introspective that selfishness is a byproduct of it existing in our hearts. Selfishness is acceptable to us when we embrace insecurity. And the worst part about it is that when we are living in that state, we hardly notice it! Yet the more we make room for God's love and correction in our hearts, the more we'll realize the need to change and have the power to change.

One of the keys to breaking bad self-esteem is to stop looking at self. Less introspection! Stop looking for the bad in you and trust in the love God has for you. Let the Lord point out the things He'd like to work on and trust His loving leading.

"Coming to Him as to a living stone, rejected indeed by men, but chosen by God and precious" (1 Peter 2:4)

Jesus lived in two realities - "rejected by man" and "chosen by God and precious." He experienced both. But He only chose to draw His identity from one. We get the same opportunity to draw our identity from the One who chose us. Sit in His Presence, open your hands and ask Him to pour out His love on you. This will destroy idolatry in our hearts.

THE CHALLENGE WITH DREAMS & DESTINY

One of the common themes of church in our day is empowering people to fulfill their dreams and destinies. Speaking identity into them and letting them know they are champions and have greatness in them.

You can even see this with many of the popular worship songs whose theme is identity. I love it and think it's important and necessary. We need it!

The challenge is to not make dreams and destiny an idol. We can actually idolize the promise of God over our lives. We become so focused on the dream and destiny it becomes more important to us than our relationship with God. There's no amount of Promised Land that can give you what the Promise Giver can.

When Israel entered into their Promised Land, each tribe had a portion given to them except the Levites. The Lord was their inheritance.

Deuteronomy 10:8-9 NIV says this: *"At that time the Lord set apart the tribe of Levi to carry the ark of the covenant of the Lord, to stand before the Lord to minister and to pronounce blessings in his name, as they still do today. That is why the Levites have no share or inheritance among their fellow Israelites; the Lord is their inheritance, as the Lord your God told them."*

The ones who were to carry the Ark were the ones who had the Lord as their inheritance. Their Promised Land was Him! He was to be more than enough for them.

Abraham was called to offer Isaac. It was the ultimate test! Abraham went through 25 years of waiting, testing and trusting in order to have the son of promise. He finally had the promise in his possession and God asked Him to sacrifice him (see Gen. 22). Right when he had the bliss of a promise fulfilled God tested him. It was an opportunity for him to not let the promise become higher in his heart than God. Perhaps this is why God had previously told Abraham that *He* was his great reward (Gen. 15:1).

Right in the midst of the agonizing raising of the knife, the Lord called out to Abraham. He told him: "...."Do not lay your hand on the lad, or do anything to him; for now I know that you fear God, since you have not withheld your son, your only son, from Me.'" (Genesis 22:12) Then Abraham looked up and there was a ram caught in the thicket. He went and grabbed that ram and offered it to God instead of his son.

I wonder if God has ever put His hand on something precious to you in your life and asked for you to let it go and give it to Him. Does Jesus still have your "yes"? Is He truly Lord of your life?

The act of obedience puts miracles in motion. God is up to something and we don't always know what's going to happen. We just follow through with obedience and trust God with the results. Abraham actually concluded that God would raise Isaac from the dead (Heb. 11:17-19). Imagine that - his faith said no matter what God will always come through!

NO PRESENCE? NO PROMISE

"Then Moses said to him, "If your Presence does not go with us, do not send us up from here. How will anyone know that you are pleased with me and with your people unless you go with us? What else will distinguish me and your people from all the other people on the face of the earth?""

(Exodus 33:15-16)

Moses was leading Israel to the Promised Land. Previously in the same chapter God told them He would send an angel to go before them but He wasn't going to go. Moses wasn't having it and basically said that the promise of God is empty without the Presence of God.

It's the opposite of what challenges this generation. Many want the promise regardless of the Presence, but Moses said "I won't have the promise without the Presence!" It means nothing without Jesus.

This isn't to say that doing what God has called and created us to do isn't satisfying. There is a fulfillment in doing God's will. That's why

Jesus said His food was to do the will of His Father and to finish His work (John 4:34). How fulfilling to lead people to Christ and see Him work miracles! We're created to do good works! (Eph. 2:10). We just function at our highest potential when Jesus is reigning on the throne of our hearts.

ALL MY PAST, ALL MY TROPHIES

Philippians 3:13 says, "but one thing I do, forgetting those things which are behind and reaching forward to those things which are ahead…"

If anyone had a past to let go of, it was the man who wrote these words. Apostle Paul was the one who persecuted Christians to their death and consented to the stoning of Stephen. I'm sure the enemy tried to mess with Paul's head by throwing his past in his face. But I love how he chose to forget what was behind him! Many of us need to do the same.

I read through Philippians 3 one day to get the full context of what Paul was saying. I realized that he wasn't writing about forgetting his past sins as much as he was saying he was forgetting his past trophies!

He wrote about how qualified he was in the Hebrew tradition: "I was circumcised when I was eight days old. I am a pure-blooded citizen of Israel and a member of the tribe of Benjamin—a real Hebrew if there ever was one! I was a member of the Pharisees, who demand the strictest obedience to the Jewish law. I was so zealous that I harshly persecuted the church. And as for righteousness, I obeyed the law without fault." (Phil. 3:5-6 NLT)

He goes on to say he considers it all trash compared to the surpassing greatness of knowing Christ! In fact, the Greek word he used to refer to his accomplishments is better translated "dung." That's a man who's rid himself of idols.

He told the Philippians - "If I wanted to put confidence in my flesh, I have a lot of reason to. In fact, I have more reason to than all of you. But I have counted them as trash and put all my confidence in Christ."

Our past sins and our trophies can actually become idols. Our past sins become an idol when we believe what we've done is greater than what Jesus did for us at the cross. Our trophies become an idol when we trust in our ability and gift more than His ability in us.

I remember hearing what Wayne Myers, apostolic missionary to Mexico, said, "A lot of people have degrees, but not many of them have temperature." It's doesn't matter how many letters you have after your name; if Jesus' Presence doesn't accompany your ministry, you need to get back on the floor and lay your life down before Him.

THE BLIND LADY

On my first mission trip outside of North America, my friends prayed for a blind lady who received her sight. We were ecstatic! We told anyone and everyone we could and rode that testimony for a long time. A couple things surprised me about the miracle.

First, I thought I had to be much further along in the faith to see something like that. One of my friends who prayed for her was only six months old in the Lord. I'm glad God began to break down that religious mindset in me.

Secondly, on the flight home, I began to feel the emotions of the moment fade away. I wanted the "high" to last forever but it was on its way out. The Lord began to speak to and showed me in Luke 10 when the disciples came back to Jesus after casting demons out. They were so excited. Jesus joined in their celebration but also redirected their joy. He told them, "…do not rejoice that the spirits submit to you, but rejoice that your names are written in heaven" (Luke 10:20 NIV).

Jesus was sinking my anchor into a deeper place. The miracles are amazing and I will continue to pursue the manifestation of the supernatural for Jesus' sake. He was speaking to me about how the emotions of an encounter would fade away, but not only am I destined for heaven, I have access to a relationship with the One who works the miracles. I can always go into my room, shut the door and meet with Him.

Bottom line is, you were created to have Jesus reign as Lord in every area of your life. This is actually how we function properly. We're stewards of what He gives us. It's time we hold our hands open to the Lord and surrender afresh. He is the One who satisfies. He is our great reward.

Carriers of the Ark live lives of surrender to Lord who is more than enough.

Questions:

- Is there anything God has highlighted to you that is taking His place in your life?

- Have you experienced the Presence of God in such a way that nothing else compares?

- Are there any things in your past (whether sins or trophies) that are holding you back? What will you do with them?

Activations:

- Take some time to worship the Lord and put words and song to the surrender present in your heart.

- Open your hands and say something like this: "Lord, I'm sitting here as the object of your love. I'm not going to try to earn anything from you right now. Father, pour out Your love on me." And just sit and receive.[4]

- Thank God for freeing you from your past sins. Take time to lay down any "trophies" that may hinder your trust in Christ.

Declarations:

- Jesus is more than enough for me. He satisfies my heart like no other.

- I receive God's unconditional love for me. Fill me up to overflowing.

- I am loved by my Father. He takes great delight in me.

- The promise of God without the Presence of God is empty. I am pursuing both!

- King Jesus reigns in my life. I put all my trust in Him.

Endnotes

1   "Enough", Words and music by Chris Tomlin and Louie Giglio, Copyright © 2002 worshiptogether.com Songs (ASCAP) sixsteps Music (ASCAP) Vamos Publishing (ASCAP) (adm. at CapitolCMGPublishing.com) All rights reserved. Used by permission.

2   Ibid.

3   The foundation for this thought process and revelation initially came from my good friend Johnson Doan who always encouraged our group that God was always thinking the very best for us.

4   The idea for this activation came from a combination of things I learned from Bill Johnson and Joseph Prince. I heard Bill share how he periodically prays a prayer very similar to this in order to keep a healthy perspective, and I read a devotional from Joseph Prince on the idea of taking "love breaks" with God; i.e. taking a "break" during your day to recieve His love.

8

PUSHING PAST BARRIERS

"If God can accept the blood as a payment for our sins
and as the price of our redemption, then we can
rest assured that the debt has been paid.
If God is satisfied with the blood, then the blood must be
acceptable… The blood [of Jesus] has satisfied God;
it must satisfy us also."
Watchman Nee, *The Normal Christian Life*

About a year and a half after I started following Jesus, I got weighed down with condemnation like crazy. I had messed up and felt too guilty and condemned to receive the truth of the gospel. It was so bad that for 2 weeks I really believed I was going to hell! The devil lied and I took it "hook, line and sinker." The weird part was that I reasoned that even though I was "going to hell" I would still live right because that's the right thing to do.

So I kept on leading worship in this small group church I was a part of. I didn't feel qualified but I did it anyway. As the Sunday night service began, I started leading worship on my guitar.

Before I could even finish the first song, God came on me in such power that I barely could strum the last chord on my guitar. Whatever devils were tormenting me got kicked off in a moment, the power of God was flowing all over me (I could feel Him physically), and I just stopped and wept. Kind of awkward when you're the worship leader trying to lead the service…but oh well, I was getting set free.

In an instant the truth that I had been meditating on from Romans 8, John 6:37, and other places just came alive in me and I believed it. It was a power encounter with the grace of God and the truth that sets us free! Service went on, but I was forever marked by His love.

If we are going to be carriers of the Ark of His Presence, the truth of the Gospel needs to be embedded into our hearts. The devil will do anything he can to get us to believe God is not for us, we aren't forgiven, we aren't qualified to carry His Presence, and the list goes on and on. He wants to stop us from entering into our full potential in Christ. Good thing we have a Savior that breaks through the enemy's lies and brings true freedom!

In this chapter, I want to focus on the battlefield of the mind and how to push past the barriers the enemy tries to set up in order to hinder us and make us feel disqualified from carrying the Ark.

WHO IS BELIAL?

One day I was reading the Bible and came across a pretty heinous story in Judges 19. I won't recount it all because of its graphic nature, but suffice to say it was reminiscent of Sodom and Gomorrah. There was wretched immorality committed, murder, and it resulted in a civil war within Israel.

The seeming perpetrators of this vile event were translated as "perverted men" in the NKJV Bible. But there was a footnote to that phrase and it said "Literally sons of Belial." I was intrigued so I did a study on where else that name shows up in the Bible.

The KJV version of the Bible translates Belial most of the time, but the modern translations give the name words like, "perverted", "corrupt", "wicked", and the like.

Here's a few samples from the Old Testament:

"**Corrupt men*** *have gone out from among you and enticed the inhabitants of their city, saying, "Let us go and serve other gods"'— which you have not known— "* (Deuteronomy 13:13, emphasis mine) *(*Lit. Sons of Belial)*

"But Hannah answered and said, "No, my lord, I am a woman of sorrowful spirit. I have drunk neither wine nor intoxicating drink, but have poured out my soul before the Lord. Do not consider your maidservant a **wicked woman***, *for out of the abundance of my complaint and grief I have spoken until now."'* (1 Samuel 1:15-16, emphasis mine) *(*Lit. daughter of Belial)*

"Now the sons of Eli were **corrupt***; *they did not know the Lord."* (1 Samuel 2:12, emphasis mine) *(*Lit. sons of Belial)*

With just a small sampling, every time Belial shows up, corruption takes place. There was not only perversion, murder and the inciting of a civil war, but people of Belial caused Israel to turn from Yahweh and serve other gods, he was known to cause drunkenness, and all the corruption that the sons of Eli engaged in - sleeping with women at the tabernacle and stealing from the offering which ultimately led the people of God astray.

That's a total of four references and we've seen a great deal of corruption! Whoever or whatever Belial is must be a root cause of corruption in society. These effects are still evident in society today.

I looked up the definition of Belial and you know what it means? "Worthlessness."

What?! You mean to tell me that one of the root causes of corruption in society is "worthlessness"?

It comes down to this: **If you believe you're worthless then you'll do worthless things.**

HOW THE SPIRIT WORLD WORKS

"Belial" is found in the Old Testament 27 times. It's in the New Testament once. Here's the reference:

> *"Do not be yoked together with unbelievers. For what do righteousness and wickedness have in common? Or what fellowship can light have with darkness? What harmony is there between Christ and Belial? Or what does a believer have in common with an unbeliever? What agreement is there between the temple of God and idols? For we are the temple of the living God..." (2 Corinthians 6:14-16 NIV)*

The Apostle Paul is contrasting opposites in this passage:

• Righteousness and wickedness.

• Light and darkness.

• Believer and unbeliever.

• Temple of God and temple of idols.

• Christ and Belial.

This not only tells us that Belial is a person, I believe a spirit, but also that whatever he does is completely the opposite of Christ.

Let me talk about spirits for a bit.

Spirits are always projecting into the environment around them whatever their assignment is. For example, if someone is dealing with a spirit of rejection, you may not even know the person, have no reason to reject them, but you just want to reject them. You choose to love them instead because you walk in love, but the enemy was trying to get you to reject them so he can stay and perpetuate the belief in the person that they are rejected...even though it's a lie.

I saw this in my youth group when I was pastoring that there could be new kids who have never met, yet if they both had drug problems, somehow by the end of the night they would find their way to each other and make friends. This also happened with the kids who were hungry for God and wanted to seek His face. They'd find each other.

When I was dating my wife, she hosted the Holy Spirit. Because she hosted the Spirit that is Holy, that Spirit was projecting into the environment around her purity and righteousness. I wasn't about to trespass in an unholy way! We used to always joke with our young people saying "there's no contact without a contract!" and "no loving it before the covenant!"

And we kept to that and remained pure. Our first official kiss was on our wedding day. It was largely due to the fact that we were walking with the Holy Spirit.

Maybe you're familiar with the phrase, "Birds of a feather flock together." That's what I'm talking about.

THE ASSIGNMENT OF CHRIST

That being said, Belial is projecting into the environment around it the lie of worthlessness. If someone chooses to agree with him, then they give a landing place to a lie and belief system that says they are worthless. And if you believe you're worthless you'll do worthless things.

At minimum, a mindset of worthlessness affects how you approach life. You approach life from a place of already being defeated and stuck in depression. It perpetuates thoughts like, "Why put effort into something if I'm not worth anything anyway?" All of the corruption mentioned earlier becomes an expression of the lack of value we feel for ourselves. It demeans our potential to live a life that is coming over and not going under. The way we approach life is essential to walking in victory.

But, oh the glorious Gospel of Jesus Christ!

If Belial's assignment is to project worthlessness onto people, then Christ is on assignment restoring people's sense of worth! It's the mission of Christ: to make sure you know how valuable you are. When that goes deep in your heart, you live in true freedom.

When Jesus came on the earth He was loving people no one wanted to love. He touched the leper that no one was allowed to touch. He welcomed the tax collectors when they had turned their backs on their own people. He loved the prostitutes with a pure love straight from His Father. Why? Because they needed to know that despite their failings, they were still worth it to Him.

This is what the Cross of Christ preaches to us. You know how much something is worth by what someone is willing to pay for it. He paid the highest price heaven could pay. Jesus gave His life for you. This changes everything. He paid for your freedom, your forgiveness, your healing, your peace and so much more. You are worthy! You are valuable! You are qualified to carry the Ark!

Did you know that Solomon's temple had so much gold and silver built into it that the estimated value of the building (only the gold and silver part) was around $15.3 billion in today's economy[1]? Apostle Paul goes on to say that we are now the temple of the Holy Spirit (1 Cor. 3:16). It's a picture of our inestimable worth.

This is how you push past the barriers. You believe the gospel. The shield of faith that quenches the fiery darts of the enemy is made up of believing what God says about us. I dare you to trust the gospel of Christ like never before.

GRACE, SIGNS & WONDERS =ANTIDOTE TO POISON

"But the unbelieving Jews stirred up the Gentiles and poisoned their minds against the brethren. Therefore they stayed there a long time, speaking boldly in the Lord, who was bearing witness to the word

of His grace, granting signs and wonders to be done by their hands." (Acts 14:2-3)

Persecution arose in the midst of the harvest and the unbelieving Jews poisoned the minds of the Gentiles. Psalm 140:3 talks about snake's poison being under the lips of the wicked. In other words, their words carried poison and it negatively affected their minds and the way they thought.

When Acts 14:3 starts with the word "therefore" we know that it is in response to verse 2. It was important for the apostles to stay and deal with the attack of the enemy. They preached the Word boldly and particularly preached the Word of His grace. God bore witness with signs and wonders. Apparently this was God's antidote to deal with the poison in their minds: grace, signs and wonders.

If you ever feel poisoned by the lies of the enemy, it's important for you to do what you can to get in an atmosphere where the grace of God is being boldly preached and demonstration of power is being released. You may even need to do it through YouTube. When you hear the Word preached under the anointing, full of faith and boldness, the power of the Word begins to break strongholds. What's even more, when God begins bearing witness to His word with signs and wonders - supernatural demonstration - it does a healing work in our minds. When we become exposed to the power of His Word and Spirit it serves as an antidote to the poison.

The manifest Presence of God coupled with the truth of His Word being preached allows us to think clearly again. The fog lifts and we can enter into the realm of the mind of Christ - much like when David played before Saul the evil spirit left and Saul felt relief. We have an even better opportunity now because we have a new creation nature that gets activated in the glory realm. It's in those moments that who we really are is activated and realized.

On a day to day basis, we have the opportunity and responsibility to renew our minds with the truth of God's Word (Rom. 12:2). The best place to do that is the manifest Presence of God.

ANITHISTAMINES

Remember when you were younger and driving in the back seat of the car with your siblings? It was hot, the AC wasn't working, and everyone seemed irritable. You finally got settled in the midst of the uncomfortable and your sibling decides they're going to put their finger an inch away from your face and say "I'm not touching you! I'm not touching you!" Then you lose your cool and blow up like a shaken soda can tossed out of a two story window.

Oh the joy. I feel stressed just writing that.

It's inevitable. When you step into being a person who carries the Presence of God, the enemy will try to do whatever he can to stop you. If you're like me, sometimes I overreact to his "flaming arrows"; those crazy thoughts he shoots at us. My overreaction actually makes it worse.

One day I was reading this passage:

"Be alert and of sober mind. Your enemy the devil prowls around like a roaring lion looking for someone to devour. Resist him, standing firm in the faith..." (1 Peter 5:8-9 NIV)

The word for "resist" in Greek is *anthistēmi.* Sounds a lot like our word antihistamine. You may already know this, but I didn't. I looked up what an antihistamine was. Simply put, an antihistamine blocks histamines. What's a histamine then?

According to WebMD, "They're chemicals your immune system makes. Histamines act like bouncers at a club. They help your body get rid of something that's bothering you..."

So why would you want to block them with an antihistamine?

"Your body's intention -- to keep you safe -- is good. But its overreaction gives you those all-too-familiar allergy symptoms, which you then try to stop with an antihistamine."[2]

Antihistamines fight an *overreaction* of histamines!

I found that whenever the enemy would shoot a thought my way - whether he was trying to remind me of some shameful thing in my past, a bad thought I had earlier that week, or put vile images in my mind - I would overreact to it just like a kid with sibling wars in the car.

I realized that's what he wanted from me - a reaction.

Some of us go into crazy spiritual warfare mode - binding, rebuking, praying in tongues wildly, pouring oil on everything, blowing a shofar and waving a flag against the devil. Not like any of those things are bad, but what we don't realize is when we overreact this way and make a bigger deal than we need to, we end up talking to the devil more than God!

Not a good plan for spiritual growth.

In the same way, some people can over-confess their sins because they didn't believe God forgave them the first time. If we do this, we can end up with more shame and guilt as a result of it. Again, because our focus is off. Shame and guilt work like barriers to keep us away from God.

When I would take my youth white water rafting for summer camps, the leaders of the camp would give instructions and guidelines for when we were on the water. If someone fell out of the boat, the first rule was "Don't panic!" It basically makes it worse and harder to get back in the boat.

Peter gave us the answer right there in 1 Peter 5:9: "Resist him, standing firm in the faith." In other words, the key to overcoming the thoughts the enemy tries to give you is don't overreact. Just like the histamines, I know you want to do good. But just don't give him the time of day. He's not worth it.

Thank Jesus for what He's done for you, repent and confess if you need to, and move forward. The shame and guilt have already been dealt with at the Cross. Jesus buried them in the grave. Don't let the devil put it back on you.

The key to not overreacting is to relax and trust in what Christ has done for you. Then move on!

Take No Thought

Did you know that in the airwaves all around you there is music, movies, tv shows, talk shows, and all kinds of entertainment? You just have to have the right equipment tuned in to the right frequency and you can pick it up. It's time to tune our hearts and minds to the frequency of truth!

I was hanging out in my house one day and the Lord said, "Take no thought." I knew it was from Matthew 6 when Jesus was teaching on worry. The phrase is used in the King James Version of the Bible.

I realized I had a choice to take whatever thought I wanted to take and make it my own.

Take no thought...that will give you a sense of defeat.

Take no thought...that will perpetuate shame in your life.

Take no thought...that devalues the Cross and emphasizes your failures.

Take no thought...that stirs up fear and doubt.

Take no thought...that says you're disqualified for God to use you.

I remember hearing Kris Vallotton say something he heard that gave him freedom: "Not every thought that comes in your head is yours."

He went on to say what I was talking about earlier in the chapter how evil spirits try to give you their thoughts. They want you to think like them so then you'll eventually act like them.

I heard Joseph Prince say once that the devil will send thoughts your way that are in the first person. For example, instead of saying, "*you're* not gonna make it", he'll say it as "*I'm* not gonna make it" so that you believe it came from you, making you the "bad guy."

This is where we don't give weight to thoughts that enter our minds that are contrary to the Word of God. Not all of the thoughts we think are ours!

But please - embrace the thoughts of truth!

Here are some thoughts to embrace:

When Jesus died on the cross, your old self died with Him.

When Jesus was buried, your old self was buried with Him.

When Jesus was raised to a new life with a new nature, your old nature was left behind, and you also came alive in Him to live a new life with a new nature, clothed in His righteousness.

When Jesus ascended and sat at the right hand of the Father because the priestly work was finished, you also were raised with Him and entered into the finished work of Christ!

"*...as He is, so are we in this world.*" (1 John 4:17)

That's the power of the gospel!

DO IT ANYWAY

Another way you push through the barriers of the enemy is to do the works of Christ regardless of how you feel.

When I was leading the young adult ministry at my church, we had outreach every Thursday in the afternoon. We actually have a university across the street so we could easily walk on campus to minister. I would meet students there and we'd set up a hand-made sign that said "Free Encouragement." Everyone wants to be encouraged. They just didn't know it was actually prophecy they were gonna get.

I would say at least 80% of the time I wasn't feeling it. Many times I would not feel anointed, qualified or ready. Good thing the Bible didn't say we walk by our feelings!

Every time we'd get there I'd just push myself past the feelings and start inviting people in to receive a free word of encouragement. You know what would happen? The River of the Spirit would start flowing and push away all those lies and contrary feelings and thoughts. Jesus said rivers of living water would flow from within us (John 7:38), and I know when those rivers flow, all the debris that's in the way gets pushed out and God moves. Clarity comes because the River pushed out the distractions.

We not only prophesied and gave words of knowledge to students passing by, we saw God heal people and pray to receive Christ!

One time, the women's basketball team was inviting us to one of their events so we took the opportunity to share with them what God was saying. The River started flowing and words of knowledge and prophecy came. It was funny because every time a new player would come up to see what was going on, they said, "Do her! Do her!" They wanted all their friends to get a word!

One of the girls ended up needing to forgive her father, so I was about to lead her into a prayer of forgiveness when I thought, let's have the whole team that's present pray with her! I thought it'd be awkward to lead her in prayer by herself so I took the opportunity to pray with the team. I did what I call an Arthur Blessit (evangelist who had led many to Christ) and had them all pray and ask God to forgive their sins!

That's the power of pushing past your feelings and doing it anyway!

You've got the Rivers of the Spirit waiting to break out and not only drive darkness away, but Holy Spirit wants to release life, healing and hope on everyone around you!

CONTRARY TO HOPE

Let me just drive this point a little bit more.

"Against all hope, Abraham in hope believed and so became the father of many nations, just as it had been said to him, "So shall your offspring be."" (Romans 4:18 NIV)

Abraham had no practical reason to believe he could have a child with his wife Sarah. They considered their bodies as good as dead! They had no qualifications to fulfill the promise of God for their lives. It had to be God!

That's why the scripture said, "Against all hope."

You may have all kinds of contrary circumstances, thoughts, past experiences, and voices all telling you there's no hope. But if Abraham could find hope, you can too. He had the promise of God and so do you.

Hope is the eager expectation that something good is coming your way. Carriers of the Ark are people who resist the temptation to give in to the hopelessness permeating their circumstances. They see beyond the temporary and contrary feelings, trust in the promise of God and move forward.

The scripture went on to say that he was fully convinced God had the power to do what He had promised. He gave glory to God.

Against all hope, Abraham in hope believed and so became.

Put your name there instead.

Against all hope, _____ in hope believed and so became.

The Power of Praise

"Complaining is to the devil what praise is to God" Jack Taylor

Psalm 8:2 says "Out of the mouth of babes and nursing infants You have ordained strength because of Your enemies, that You may silence the enemy and the avenger."

Yet when Jesus quoted that verse in Matthew 21:16 He said, "'Out of the mouth of babes and nursing infants You have perfected praise'". Jesus interpretation of "ordained strength" came out as "perfected praise." Praise and strength are synonymous. Praise brings strength into your life.

We also see that childlike praise silences the enemy!

2 Chronicles 20 documents one of the most powerful references to praise in the Bible. Long story short, the strategy King Jehoshaphat used to fight the battle was praise. The enemy ended up fighting against each other and defeating themselves! Confusion was sent into the enemy's camp because they forgot who they were fighting and fought against themselves.

Therein are at least three different benefits of praise:

• It brings strength
• It silences the enemy
• It sends confusion to the enemy's camp

Complaining on the other hand is the inverse of praise. It saps our strength, amplifies the enemy's influence in our lives, and brings confusion in our identity and destiny. The sword God gave us gets turned on us and reaps havoc. We end up defeating ourselves!

As people who are called to carry the Ark, we need to keep our focus right. Praising God is one of the best ways to do it. When the priests carried the Ark into Jerusalem, they were surrounded by exuberant praise! (1 Chron. 15:15)

If you really want to push through the barriers, it's time you lifted your voice and gave thanks and praise to the Lord! You can praise above the attacks. When you do, you are enforcing the victory of the Cross that disarmed the enemy (Psalm 149:6-9, Col. 2:15), you cut off his influence in your life, and you send confusion into his camp! His lies lose their power in the midst of genuine praise.

Praise will restore clarity in your identity and destiny, put strength back in you and shut the enemy up!

GETTIN' SHIGGY WITH IT

Let me go a little further on praise.

"A prayer of Habakkuk the prophet, on Shigionoth." (Habakkuk 3:1)

The prophet was going through a rough time as he wrote this. You can see at the end of the chapter his summary, that even though things aren't going well, he chose to rejoice in God. The last phrase of the chapter reads "To the Chief Musician. With my stringed instruments." So we know this was more than a prayer, it was a song to be sung.

But what many people don't notice is this word "shigionoth." It's a musical term. It told the musicians how to play the song. It means "strong emotion, impassioned triumph."

The AMPC Bible translated it this way:

"A prayer of Habakkuk the prophet, set to wild, enthusiastic, and triumphal music."

This is the kind of praise that defies the circumstance.

You'd expect that Habakkuk would write a sad country song in the midst of his trial. But he completely defies the circumstance and writes a song that is meant to be wild, passionate and triumphant!

The enemy's goal in any trial is to get us to give in to apathy. Apathy is defined as the suppression or absence of passion. Shigionoth is praise that resists the spirit of heaviness! It says, "There may be a storm *around* me, but it's not getting *in* me! I will praise God with a triumphant passion!"

Thus the barriers are broken through and you move into Kingdom impact.

LOOK UP

In Numbers 21, Israel was going through a pretty rough time. Here's a summary:

- One of their leaders just died (Aaron)
- Moses just heard that he wasn't allowed to go into the Promised Land
- Edom didn't let them travel through their land, making them have to take a longer, more difficult route
- The King of Arad comes against them
- They're 38 years into their wilderness journey

Wow. That's a tough time.

Israel starts complaining and even goes so far to call the miracle manna bread worthless! God sent fiery serpents against them and people start dying from snake bites. They end up repenting to Moses and Moses prays to God.

> *"Then the LORD said to Moses, "Make a fiery serpent, and set it on a pole; and it shall be that everyone who is bitten, when he looks at it, shall live." So Moses made a bronze serpent, and put it on a pole; and so it was, if a serpent had bitten anyone, when he looked at the bronze serpent, he lived."*(Numbers 21:8-9)

The only thing the people had to do was look up! In other words, the miracle was released when they changed their focus! My good friend Jerame Nelson always says, "What you focus on you empower." It's the key to pushing past barriers.

What's more is that Jesus said that serpent was a foreshadowing of Himself:

"And as Moses lifted up the serpent in the wilderness, even so must the Son of Man be lifted up, that whoever believes in Him should not perish but have eternal life." (John 3:14-15)

It's a picture of the finished work of Christ at the cross! Bronze representing judgment and the serpent representing the sting of our sin. Jesus took our judgment and sin at the cross so we could be free, forgiven and healed!

It's time to look up at Jesus and what He's done for you! He's the One who qualifies you. See Him! Your miracle and breakthrough is found in taking your eyes off yourself and looking to Christ!

Take time to meditate on the majesty and mercy of the Person of Christ. Get caught up in gazing upon Him. It's actually nourishment for your mind and heart to behold Him. Jesus said Himself that whoever feeds on Him will live (John 6:57).

This is actually one of the best ways to defeat dark thoughts - behold Jesus.

In Conclusion

"For the weapons of our warfare are not physical [weapons of flesh and blood], but they are mighty before God for the overthrow and destruction of strongholds, [Inasmuch as we] refute arguments and theories and reasonings and every proud and lofty thing that sets itself up against the [true] knowledge of God; and we lead every

thought and purpose away captive into the obedience of Christ (the Messiah, the Anointed One)"

(2 Corinthians 10:4-5 AMPC)

It's the arguments, theories, reasonings, and the prideful thoughts that we get to take captive to the obedience of Christ. We prove wrong the lies with the truth of God's word. As we behold Jesus and trust in His word, strongholds begin to crumble.

We all go through times of attack and testing. I'm grateful for the glorious gospel of Jesus Christ that empowers us to move forward through it all! We've got God given tools to push past every barrier the enemy puts in our way.

Let's move into all that God has for us as we carry the Ark of His Presence!

Questions:

- What was God highlighting to you as you read this chapter?
- Identify the main areas the enemy tries to use against you. What does God have to say about that?
- What is God asking you to believe right now, regardless of how you feel?

Activations:

- Write a list of scriptural things that God says about you in the areas you're needing breakthrough in. Declare them over yourself daily for a week.
- One way to exercise your rest and trust in Christ is to laugh. God sits in heaven and laughs at the enemy (Ps. 2:4). Next time you get a crazy thought, try laughing it off.
- Take a 5 minute praise break. Get shiggy with it!

Declarations:

- God paid the highest price for me. I am valuable and worthy.
- I rest in the finished work of Christ.
- Not every thought that comes in my head is from me. I trust in what God says about me.
- I am anointed by God, I am qualified to be used by God, and I believe His Word regardless of how I feel.
- I will praise the Lord with an impassioned triumph in all circumstances.
- The Rivers of the Spirit flow from within me releasing life, healing and hope on those all around me.

Endnotes
1   Randall Price, ThM, PhD, Rose Guide to the Temple (Carson, CA: Rose Publishing, Inc.) p. 24
2   https://www.webmd.com/allergies/what-are-histamines#1

9

SURRENDER TO THE FLOW

"Aslan is a lion- the Lion, the great Lion." "Ooh" said Susan. "I'd
thought he was a man. Is he-quite safe? I shall feel rather nervous
about meeting a lion"..."Safe?" said Mr Beaver ..."Who said
anything about safe? 'Course he isn't safe.
But he's good. He's the King, I tell you."
C.S. Lewis, *The Lion, the Witch and the Wardrobe*

Years ago, I went with my church on a mission trip to Uganda, Africa to preach the gospel. It was such a powerful trip as we saw hundreds give their lives to Christ, the sick were healed - with at least 2 crippled people walking, and people delivered from darkness. God moved!

We usually have a "fun day" at the end of our trips, so we planned to go river rafting on the Nile River. I had actually gotten sick the night before, and, putting it nicely, I was losing liquids all night long. My body was drained of strength and wasn't fully prepared to paddle down Class 5 rapids (which, by the way, is the highest class of rapids you're allowed to go on with a raft). So I was planning to just hang out at the dock and relax.

That's when the guides and some of our team came over and worked to persuade me to go. They told me that there was a "wild" ride and a "mild" ride. Plus, the boat that had all the girls (which included my future wife) needed a lead paddler. And they were taking the "mild" ride.

I mean, how bad could it be?

It started out great.

After all, I had done this before with my youth group so it wasn't entirely new. Except that was a river in Northern California. This was Africa.

Everything changed when we hit this Class 5 rapid. The raft turned around and I lost grip of my paddle, it hit me in the head, I started bleeding and fell out of the raft! I was floating down the Nile River thinking this could be my last moments on earth.

It felt like the old cartoons where the character would be drowning and every few moments you'd hear them bubble out a yelp for help. Lol.

I wasn't drowning, but I sure was panicking. (Should've read the last chapter…) Finally, a guy on a kayak came and picked me up and brought me to shore. I was ready to go home. The raft made its way over to me and the guide basically said, "You can't go home because we're in the middle of the river. The only way out is to finish up the course."

Noooooo!

We made it through and I managed to stay in the raft for the rest of the trip. I found out later that the only difference between the "wild" and "mild" ride was that on the "wild" ride they flipped the raft on purpose! It was the same rapids the whole time!

Lord have mercy.

Oh, and they also told me that the place where we rafted was one of the highest concentrated places of witchcraft in the area.

Thanks guys.

Rivers can get wild and so can surrendering to the flow of the Spirit.

I'm not talking about bleeding, near death experiences, and witchcraft...I'm talking about the life that comes from surrendering to the Spirit. It's just like when Mr. Beaver, from "The Lion, The Witch, and The Wardrobe" talks about Aslan the Lion and says, "'Course he isn't safe. But he's good."[1]

EZEKIEL'S VISION

In Ezekiel 47:1-12, the prophet has a vision of water flowing from the temple. It's a picture of the River of the Spirit.

The angel speaking with him takes him one thousand cubits in and he's up to his ankles. Then goes even further and goes up to his knees. Even further, and he's up to his waist. Then finally, he goes even deeper, and he was unable to touch the floor anymore. He had to surrender to the flow!

It's a picture of the Christian moving into deeper realms of the Spirit.

Notice you still have control when you're ankle, knee and waist deep. You've got more of the River but still maintaining control. God wants to take you deeper and cause you to surrender to the flow of wherever the River takes you.

This can happen for worship leaders when Holy Spirit wants to take the song further than what was originally written. For preachers when the Lord decides He'd like to preach something other than what their notes say. For everyday believers who are sensitive to the leading of the Spirit when He wants to move in a certain direction.

Being carriers of the Ark requires us to let go of control and let Holy Spirit do what He wants to do. This calls for sensitivity and friendship with the Holy Spirit.

Crazy, Unsure, or Offended

I remember the first time our youth and young adult groups encountered a "fire tunnel." If you don't know what that is, people form two lines that make a tunnel type walkway, and then others come through it for prayer, impartation, and a touch from Heaven.

We had really been pushing in to the deeper things of the Spirit and this was a great way to go further…except for the fact that people were freaked out. There were all kinds of manifestations like falling, shaking, laughing, and rolling on the ground. We had to carry two of the girls back to the car because they got so drunk in the Spirit they couldn't walk.

Our group was split up in three groups:

- The Crazy (who were getting blasted in the fire tunnel)
- The Unsure (who stood nearby the fire tunnel watching with a look that said "hmmmm?")
- The Offended (who stood afar off from the fire tunnel with their arms crossed and angry faces).

I got to be the pastor!

Yay.

We had been comfortable with prophetic words and occasional healings, but this…this was too crazy for us…at least some of us. Apparently we signed up for the "mild" ride and got duped.

It was the dividing line for those who wanted more of God no matter the cost. There's no "mild" version of Pentecost. If you want more of the Spirit, you've got to go deeper in the River. The deeper you go the more surrender is required.

This doesn't mean you'll have to shake, rattle and roll, but I'm sure it'll take you out of your comfort zone.

I FOUND IT IN THE BIBLE

This led me to search the scripture for answers. I won't do an entire study here, but suffice to say, when Psalm 16:11 says in God's Presence is fullness of joy, you can't exclude wild exuberant expressions of joy because of fear and misunderstanding.

Unusual signs and wonders began to manifest especially as we became a part of the Fire & Glory Outpouring in San Diego. Many of the things in scripture I took as metaphors were starting to happen in the natural and my way of understanding was challenged and stretched.

When manna started to appear for Israel in the wilderness it was something new and fresh. They actually named it "manna" because they didn't know what it was! Manna means "what is it?" People criticize when they see unusual signs and wonders, but they don't realize God has been doing this kind of stuff for thousands of years.

I realized I was trying to get God to be made in my image rather than me being formed in His. I wanted Him to be tame, comfortable and easy to understand but that's just not how it works. He's God and I am not.

After teaching the Word and pushing for more of the Spirit, our kids ended up being one of the most wild youth groups I've ever known. They worshiped God with passion, could pray and prophesy, some were releasing healing on their campus and they manifested like crazy people!

One time we were in a Jesus Culture conference and our group happened to be some of the craziest there. Some of my youth sat in front of a Lutheran youth group and during worship they decided to turn around and pray for them. Two kids got the gift of tongues for the first time, two other kids got hit with the joy of the Lord and then another girl was manifesting a demon.

The only reason I knew was because my wife and I went out to the lobby to check on a kid who never returned from the bathroom and I see them trying to cast the demon out of this girl!

No joke, my youth were manifesting so wildly, that we had someone come up to one of our youth leaders and say how nice it was that we brought the autistic kids to the conference! No offense, but I want you to get the picture. I had to teach them how to simmer down and sit calmly so they could listen to the messages being preached.

DETHRONE YOUR MIND

Wild manifestations and unusual signs and wonders are some of the things God uses to help us dethrone our minds. It doesn't have to be wild and crazy all the time in order for it to be God. Wild manifestations aren't the tell-all sign of spiritual maturity. But they *are* one of the things God uses to shake us up, help us lighten up, and offend our minds. God wants to offend our minds because He doesn't want our understanding to take lead.

"Trust in the Lord with all your heart, and lean not on your own understanding;" (Proverbs 3:5)

This doesn't mean we don't use our brains. This just means we don't let our understanding take a higher place than our trust in God. Remember it's about surrendering to the flow of the Spirit.

This also doesn't mean we move away from the scripture. We're like the person depicted in Psalm 1 that is like a tree planted by the rivers of water. There's the River again! We're planted in truth and get our life from the Spirit.

It happened to the disciples in John 6. Jesus started preaching that people needed to eat His flesh and drink His blood. Not exactly the "ideal message" for building a church. Check out some of the disciple's response:

*"Therefore many of His disciples, when they heard this, said, "This is a hard saying; who can **understand** it? When Jesus knew in Himself that His disciples complained about this, He said to them, "Does this offend you? What then if you should see the Son of Man ascend where He was before? It is the Spirit who gives life; the flesh profits nothing. The words that I speak to you are spirit, and they are life...From that time many of His disciples went back and walked with Him no more."* (John 6:60-63, 66, emphasis mine)

Notice the issue was with *understanding*. Jesus was speaking on a deeper level. His words are spirit and they are life.

"Then Jesus said to the twelve, "Do you also want to go away?" But Simon Peter answered Him, "Lord, to whom shall we go? You have the words of eternal life." (John 6:67-68)

People were offended because they didn't understand. But Jesus was teaching His disciples how to listen on a deeper level. Their minds weren't able to comprehend but their spirit could sense His life. God wants to teach us how to listen and discern by the Spirit. It's the Spirit who gives life; the flesh profits nothing.

SPIRITUAL PERCEPTION

As I travel, I notice many people haven't learned how to live from their spirit. We are a spirit, we have a soul and we live in a body (1 Thess. 5:23). We're made in the image of God and God is Spirit (John 4:24). Our spirit is the most real part of us. It should be where we live from.

Even John the Baptist as a baby in his mother's womb could perceive Jesus in Mary's womb when she walked into the room (Luke 1:41). His brain wasn't fully formed yet, but his spirit man was alive! He could perceive the anointing of the Anointed One!

It was the same with Simeon and Anna when baby Jesus is brought into the temple to be dedicated. I'm sure there were more babies than

Jesus coming into the temple at that time, but they had enough friendship with Holy Spirit to know the difference (Luke 2:25-38).

Again, later on, Peter answered Jesus' question, "Who do you say that I am?" with a right-on revelation from the Father (Matt. 16:16). All by spiritual perception.

Carriers of the Ark are the kind of people who have taken time to practice and be trained to know the voice and moving of the Spirit. Not merely head knowledge, but revelation borne out of friendship and intimacy with God.

There are times when I'll be doing errands publicly and I start feeling the power of God in my hand. That's when I know to start looking for someone that needs healing because the anointing to heal just showed up. Or it could simply be the inner witness or drawing of the Holy Spirit.

Other times I feel heat in certain areas of a room or sense an angel there. One time we were waiting to go into a service as the band was practicing, and I sensed an angel of fire standing right by the doorway. I told one of our young adults to go stand there and as soon as she did she fell to the ground under the power of God.

Another time I saw Jesus pointing to the back of this lady at a breakfast table in a hotel we were staying at. I asked her if she needed healing there and she did, so my wife and I prayed for her. She felt the heat of the Holy Spirit and was healed!

When I'm leading worship or preaching, I'll have something prepared, but I always hold it loosely based on the flow of the Holy Spirit. We've gone into so many amazing moments of revelation and God encounters because of the leading of the Lord and not holding so tight to the plan. What's more, this can still happen within the boundaries of time constraints!

Even outside of ministry contexts, my heart is always open to listen to the Lord. That's Proverbs 3:6: "In all your ways acknowledge Him,

And He shall direct your paths." "Acknowledge" in the Hebrew means to know intimately. In other words, carry your friendship with God into everything and He'll show you the way.

My wife and I will even practice by turning off the GPS and ask Holy Spirit how to get wherever we're going! We want to learn His voice more and more! Plus, it's fun!

This is Hebrews 5:14 NASB: "But solid food is for the mature, who **because of practice** have their senses **trained** to discern good and evil." (emphasis mine)

PARALLEL DECEPTION

During that same time in our youth and young adult groups, the haters were still present. Someone brought up the name of some Hindu god and said that all the laughing and shaking looked like a video they saw on YouTube of Hindus and since it looked like it, it must be it. The conclusion was that we're in error.

Again, I'm searching scripture and listening for what God wanted to say about that.

He began to speak to me about what I call "parallel deception." The enemy takes something good from the kingdom and copies it. Then when good intending Christians see that darkness does the same thing, they lose interest and even reject the original because it might be the devil. You may be familiar with the phrase, "Don't throw the baby out with the bathwater."

The devil loves to take powerful things from the kingdom and put something parallel to it. That way, you end up throwing the whole thing out instead of separating the two. This happens with things like manifestations, joy & laughter, signs & wonders, and many of the supernatural demonstrations that God does. It's the enemy's way of discrediting the real gifts of the Kingdom. The problem is when you do that you're left with dead religion.

It comes from Acts 16:16-18. There was a young girl who had a demon who allowed her to tell the future. The weird part was, she was saying about Apostle Paul and Silas, "These men are servants of the Most High God, who proclaim to us the way of salvation." Sounds right...but something was off.

Even though she was saying the right thing, something was off with her spirit.

We need spiritual perception to discern the parallel deception.

Imagine now, you're preaching the gospel in a town that needs Jesus and the fortune teller is preaching the same message. People may be asking, "What's the difference between you and her? Your messages are the same!" It was the devil's tactic to discredit the salvation message Paul and Silas were preaching.

Paul got agitated and cast the demon out of her. He was able to discern the spirit of this girl.

If we have friendship with Holy Spirit, we'll be able to tell the difference. I said this earlier, but many people are more convinced of the devil's ability to deceive them than they are convinced of God's ability to keep them. Greater is He that is within you! Trust your Friend to tell you the truth and show you the scripture.

Just because it may look the same as something the devil is doing doesn't mean it's the devil (remember when the magicians copied all the miracles Moses did in Pharaoh's court? Ex. 7:8-13). He got it from God in the first place. God is the Creator. The devil can only counterfeit. Also, offense isn't the same thing as spiritual discernment. We've got to know the difference! Just because something offends your theology doesn't mean it's not God.

CULTIVATE FRIENDSHIP

"The amazing grace of the Master, Jesus Christ, the extravagant love of God, the intimate friendship of the Holy Spirit, be with all of you." (2 Corinthians 13:14 MSG)

Holy Spirit is a person. Yes, He's depicted as a River, a Dove, a Fire, a Wind, etc. But the bottom line is, He is a Person and He is just as much God as the Father is and the Son is. According to this passage, we can have an intimate friendship with Him.

Don Potter opens his book on worship with this:

"After leading praise in a church for many years, the Lord stopped me in the middle of a song and said, "I want you to go home and praise Me until you learn to truly sense My presence."[2]

I love how when God walked into the Garden of Eden, Adam and Eve knew it. The Bible didn't say they *saw* Him, it said they *heard* the sound of the Lord God walking (Gen. 3:8). They knew when God walked in. They knew His sound, His frequency, His nearness. Do you know Him like that?

Can you sense the shift in the atmosphere during worship times when Jesus moves in more mightily? When He begins to set up His throne upon the praise? Or when God decides to manifest His Presence in your home prayer times? Or just reveals His Presence in your day to day life?

And do you know how to keep Him there? I know the theology that He is always with us and will never leave us. But I'm talking about sustaining the manifest Presence of God.

This comes from intimacy and friendship with God. Even using those phrases seem too limited for what I'm trying to communicate. It's beyond logic, it's beyond reason; it's Spirit to spirit connection with the Living God. That's why the gift of tongues is so valuable. You communicate on a deeper level than your mind can comprehend.

This is at least one of the reasons David made what is known as "David's Tabernacle" (1 Chron. 16:1-4). He knew what it was to entertain the Presence of the King. To minister unto Him. To invoke the pleasure of God. It was what he did in the shepherd fields before he was anointed king. It was that quality that attracted God to him and choose him to be king. David was a man after God's own heart. It's a heart that's fully surrendered and fully satisfied.

Paul said it like this: "What is more, I consider everything a loss because of the surpassing worth of knowing Christ Jesus my Lord, for whose sake I have lost all things. I consider them garbage, that I may gain Christ" (Phil. 3:8 NIV). This is where it all begins and ends - knowing Him.

We've got to fight the propensity to be a "good Christian." Just have relationship with God. Eternal life is to know Him (John 17:3). Hang out with Him and ask Him questions. Read the scripture and fill your mind and heart with His words. Pray in tongues as much as you can. Give Him praise and worship every day. Not because of religious duty, but because of genuine relationship. And watch as He responds and reveals Himself to you.

FUNNER, CA

Recently, as I've been driving around Southern California, I keep noticing these signs for Harrah's Casino located in Funner, CA. I wasn't sure if that was a real city or not, so I Googled it and found it was! The city was made official in August 2016. It basically covers the 40 acres of the casino's facility.

To take it even further, they made the first mayor of the city David Hasselhoff! All of this was an idea from an advertising agency "to reflect the resort's mission to help raise the level of visitor "fun" to an even higher level" said Andrew Levine in Forbes magazine.[3]

What an idea! What if the church had that much of a fun level?!

Now I know that "fun" isn't the first thing most people think of when they think of church, but what if there was so much life flowing that church was the first place people thought of when looking for a good time?

Yes, I get it. Church should have some reverence and holiness to it...but remember the River?

"There is a river whose streams make glad the city of God..."

(Psalm 46:4)

The River makes glad! The word for "make glad" means "to cause to rejoice, gladden, probably to brighten up, to make blithe, gleesome."

And "blithe" means: joyous, merry, or happy in disposition; glad, cheerful; without thought of regard; carefree; heedless.[4]

I'm pretty sure church could use more of that! And it all comes from the River!

When's the last time your worship experience included a dance party full of joy? When's the last time God showed up so powerfully you ended up doing what my wife and I call the "laugh-cry"? (Where God is so good you want to cry but end up laughing hysterically at the same time).

When is the last time the River was flowing so strong that you became carefree and just rejoiced in God?

This is the power of surrendering to the flow!

One of the things I've appreciated about working with Jerame & Miranda Nelson at the Fire & Glory Outpouring in San Diego is the amount of fun we have. God is moving in radical healings, signs and wonders, prophetic is flowing strong, reverence and holiness are exemplified, the nations are literally being touched by the Spirit of revival - but we also have a lot of fun! People get pleasantly surprised when we break out in freestyle rapping during the worship times!

Someone once said that "Seriousness is not a fruit of the Spirit, but joy is!"

That's how you know you've been surrendering to the flow - there's joy. People have lightened up, tension is loosened, and there's a sense of freedom. Remember, when you're flowing down the River, you're not striving, you're surrendering.

Deeper Than Hype

It's not hype! It's rejoicing on a deeper level. It's Psalm 42:7 that says "deep calls unto deep."

As I mentioned earlier, I've found that it's much harder for people to break out in rejoicing and dancing for the Lord than it is for them to sing a slower song and cry. There's this weird idea that the fast songs are just the warm up songs and they're not "real" worship. It's the idea that says "once we get to the slow songs, then I'll really press in and it'll be real worship."

Not only do we enter into God's courts with praise and thanksgiving, but the Bible also said in His Presence is fullness of joy! It's all filled with joy from start to end! When David and the people brought the Ark of the Covenant to Jerusalem, it was a joyful dance party! (1 Chron. 15:16, 25, 2 Sam. 6:12-16).

David's wife Michal, the daughter of Saul, despised him when she saw him dancing with all his might before the Lord. The scripture tells us that she had no children to the day of her death. It didn't say she was barren, it just said that she had no children - which points to the fact that she lost intimacy with David. She was married to the king yet had no intimacy. There's a realm of intimacy that we miss out on when we despise joy. Jesus is anointed with the oil of joy!

Michal's name by definition means "a little stream of water." You know by now that we were meant to have rivers of living water flowing from within us! Don't settle for just a little stream. Carriers of the Ark are people who know how to have fun and rejoice on a deeper level than the world's hype! We've got joy!

WHAT'S AT STAKE?

Why flow? Because when you do what God wants to do, His life and Presence are on it. And if His life and Presence are on it, then transformation happens in people's lives. Not only that, but we are put back into our natural habitat; the atmosphere for which we were created, which is the Presence of God.

Jesus didn't die to start a religion. Jesus died so that we could have reconnected relationship with the Father. So the reason we need to surrender to the flow is so that His life is found in everything we do. If not, we may come under the risk of having a form of godliness yet denying its power (2 Tim. 3:5).

This is what is at stake. We want Holy Spirit to have his way.

It's His church, the people are His people, the word is His word, it's His breath in our lungs and everything we have came from Him in the first place. So it's fitting that He would have His way. Not that we don't have any part in it, it's just that what He has to give is so much better and actually brings life. Remember, Jesus said the flesh profits nothing.

What are we doing if there is no anointing, no fresh breath of the Spirit, no words from heaven or God's presence manifest?

May it never be said that our program can freely continue if God removed His presence. Jesus didn't give His life for that and He doesn't expect you to either. But it's His love in the relationship He offers that I would gladly give my life for.

It's time to get in the River and see where He takes you! The supernatural power, love, and joy of God await you!

Questions:

- Are there areas in your life that need to surrender to the flow?

- Where have you let your understanding take lead over your trust in God?

- How does God usually speak to you?

Activations:

- Worship leaders: Take one of your songs out of your set to make time for the flow of the Spirit. Sing and play what He is doing.

- Take time to listen to the Holy Spirit as you go through your day. See if He'd like you to talk or pray with someone.

- Take an extra 15mins before your day to worship, pray and wait on the Lord. Ask Him to show you anything for the day ahead.

Declarations:

- I am the most sensitive person to the Holy Spirit.

- I am growing in my sensitivity and intimacy with the Holy Spirit.

- I lean not on my own understanding. I trust in God first.

- I make time to read, study, and meditate on the Word of God.

- The Presence of God is the most valuable thing to me.

- I surrender to the flow of what God wants to do. He is the Lord.

- The joy of the Lord is my strength.

Endnotes

1   C.S. Lewis, The Lion, the Witch, and the Wardrobe (New York, NY: Harper-Collins Publishers) p. 86

2   Don Potter, Facing the Wall (Moravian Falls, NC: Potterhaus Music) p. 7

3   https://www.forbes.com/sites/andrewlevine2/2017/05/24/the-curious-case-of-funner-california/#36deb8e81d2c

4   https://www.dictionary.com/browse/blithe?s=t

10

PORTABLE PRESENCE CARRIERS

"The glory is always broadcasting"
Mahesh Chavda

Maybe you've seen the old Indiana Jones movie, "Raiders of the Lost Ark". Remember when they opened the Ark and people's faces literally melted? As much as I'd like to have a guitar solo that does that, I don't think God wants to melt people's faces off. I do believe, however, that we have a supernatural God who still does astounding miracles.

I did some research about the Ark of the Covenant and found some interesting things. Just for fun, check this out. The Jewish Virtual Library says about the ark, "According to one midrash, it would clear the path for the nation by burning snakes, scorpions, and thorns with two jets of flame that shot from its underside (*T. VaYakhel*, 7)".[1] That's amazing! Talk about a protection plan. It reminds me of Psalm 97:3 that says: "A fire goes before Him, and burns up His enemies round about."

We know that when Joshua led Israel into the Promised Land, the Lord instructed that the priests carry the ark into the Jordan River.

When they did that, as soon as their feet touched the water, the river was supernaturally pulled back very far away. All of Israel then crossed over on dry ground. That's a demonstration of supernatural power for sure, but check out this verse:

> *"It came about when the priests who carried the ark of the covenant of the Lord had come up from the middle of the Jordan, and* **the soles of the priests' feet were lifted up to the dry ground**, *that the waters of the Jordan returned to their place, and went over all its banks as before."*

(Joshua 4:18 NASB, emphasis mine)

Another midrash (rabbinical commentary) said that the ark carried its carriers by lifting them up off the ground and carrying them to the shore of the Jordan. In the verse above, the priests feet were said to have been "lifted up" (the verb tense being passive). The rabbis interpreted that as the ark actually carrying those who carried it.

That same midrash goes on to say that was the reason why Uzza got struck dead. He reached out to touch the ark because the oxen pulling the cart it was placed on had stumbled. The implication being that he was trying to keep the ark from falling. The rabbi wrote, "The Holy One, Blessed be He, said to him: Uzza, the Ark carried its bearers when it crossed the Jordan; all the more so is it not clear that it can carry itself?"[2]

Wow. Fire coming out and destroying enemies, priests being lifted up off the ground supernaturally, parting a river and drying up ground! We know the parting of the Jordan was legit, but whether those other things are true or not, you can be the judge. I just think it's pretty cool and expands my viewpoint of what I think is possible with God.

When Jesus was born, He was the Ark of the covenant in the flesh. He "tabernacled" amongst us as John 1:14 says. In the Old Testament, the Ark dwelt in a tent. In Jesus' day, He was the Ark in the tent of His body. Now today, we've become Carriers of the Ark as Christ has made

His home in us - "Christ in you, the hope of glory." (Col. 1:27) We are portable presence carriers!

If that same Presence is within us and upon us today, what are the possibilities?

Carriers of the Ark are people who change atmospheres. They know the life-giving power of God's Presence is not just reserved for services or meetings. They walk with Jesus in their day to day lives. This glory they carry translates into love for souls. They supernaturally impact the world around them because they carry the King of kings on their shoulders.

THE ATMOSPHERE WE CARRY

As mentioned multiple times, the first time David tried to bring in the Ark it was unsuccessful in a way. Yet we see something very powerful take place as the Ark was temporarily placed at a nearby house. By way of unintentionality of man, the ark of the Lord came to stay at Obed-Edom's house.

The Bible records it like this:

"The ark of the Lord remained in the house of Obed-Edom the Gittite three months. And the Lord blessed Obed-Edom and all his household.

Now it was told King David, saying, "The Lord has blessed the house of Obed-Edom and all that belongs to him, because of the ark of God." So David went and brought up the ark of God from the house of Obed-Edom to the City of David with gladness." (2 Samuel 6:11-12)

The blessing of the Lord got on him, his household and all that belonged to him because he hosted the ark for three months! He just happened to be at the right place at the right time. Blessing is attached to the Presence! The atmosphere of the Lord carries within it the necessary components for blessing, abundance and prosperity. Everything that he had got blessed. Presence carries life with it and things just supernaturally thrive there.

For Obed-Edom, I'm sure his cattle, his crops, and his grass came to life! His wife probably got pregnant with twins and the already existing kids probably got scholarships to the best rabbi university around! What I'm trying to say is: it wasn't just internal blessing, people were talking about it. It must've been seen! The blessing affects our spirit and soul as well as everything that belongs to us.

The Presence of God is the atmosphere that all good things thrive in. This is what we carry.

PERPETUAL SPRINGTIME

My wife and I bought a house a few years ago, and as all homeowners discover, there's a lot more work to it than when you're renting. You can't call the maintenance guy anymore because you are the maintenance guy now! One thing we inherited was a garden with roses and fruit trees. But we didn't move in until November, so winter was well on its way in, and that means everything goes dormant - even in beautiful Southern California.

Spring time finally came around and I began to see colors and plants come to life all over my back yard. I saw things that I didn't know were there like a section of garlic and onion plants that started to sprout in a place I thought was just barren soil. The roses came to life and let off such an amazing fragrance in the air. Fruit trees grew leaves and flowers and the bees got to work. It was like a whole ecosystem came to life once spring arrived.

This is Song of Solomon 2:11-12: "For lo, the winter is past, The rain is over and gone. The flowers appear on the earth; The time of singing has come, And the voice of the turtledove is heard in our land." The root word for winter in Hebrew means to hide. It was not only a season shift from winter to spring, but from hiding to breaking forth.

The Lord began to speak to me about what the Presence of Jesus brings forth in our lives. Jesus was the glory of God in flesh. When people got around Him they came alive! People were released in to their destinies! The sick were healed, the people were forgiven, the dead were literally raised! People who society had written off and driven away as outcasts were welcomed in and given purpose. Things that were dormant and dead came alive when Jesus came on the scene. Jesus is perpetual springtime!

The blessing at Obed-Edom's house was a foreshadowing of what Jesus would do when He came.

He came to bring life in abundance! He released it everywhere He went. In His Presence champions are released, layers of guilt and shame are lifted, and people come alive. It's where clarity comes and callings are discovered.

Our new creation nature comes forth in the glory. Who we truly are gets activated. We begin to see what we were created for, the mind of Christ flows freely, and the love of God overflows from us. Being around Jesus truly brings out the best in you.

Jesus is called the Dayspring, or Sunrise, the Sun of Righteousness, the Bright and Morning Star. He is the dawning of a new day. He is our change from night to day. He is the release from darkness. He is the Light of the world. And when He rises in people's lives, as Malachi prophesied, healing comes and they are released from their limitations!

SOME THINGS CAN'T SURVIVE

It's also important to note that not everything can survive in the glory. In the Presence of God certain things come to life and other things die. In Obed-Edom's house I think it looked like the weeds that died, barrenness died, and lack died. In Jesus' day, He cast out devils, cursed the fig tree, rebuked the Pharisees, calmed the storm, and corrected His disciples. In Mark 1:24, the demon in a man could not stand to be in the Presence of Jesus any longer that it had to manifest and Jesus cast it out immediately. Some things just can't survive in His atmosphere.

When climbing a high mountain, there's need for acclimation so you can survive at a higher altitude. Your body needs to adjust to the lower levels of oxygen. When climbing Mount Everest, you have to go up and then back down multiple times in order to acclimate. Then there's what's known as the "death zone" which is the last 4,000 ft. to the summit. That's because after 25,000 ft. in elevation your body actually begins to die because of the low oxygen levels. Mount Everest is 29,029 ft. in elevation, making it the highest peak in the world. Some people use oxygen tanks just to make it to the top for a short period of time.[3] The higher you go, some things just can't survive.

Just like that, when we ascend the hill of the Lord and stand in His Presence, some things come to life: destiny, purpose, hope, identity, lives, marriages, wisdom, health, gifts, and all things kingdom. Yet other things die: fear, shame, guilt, condemnation, slander, stress, depression, lies, etc. As carriers of His Presence, it's like two birds get hit with one stone. While the works of the flesh get destroyed, the purpose of God gets fulfilled.

Sanctification happens here. It's also a great opportunity for mind renewal. This is where acclimation comes in. We can acclimate to higher heights in the Spirit.

More Glory

It's God's will for us that we go from one degree of glory to another. One translation says an ever-increasing glory (2 Cor. 3:18 NIV). In order to do that, we need to acclimate! Higher heights can also mean more weighty glory. In Chapter 5, I shared the story of Smith Wigglesworth and the weighty glory that would come when he prayed. So much so that pastors would leave the room because they couldn't handle it. One of the Hebrew words for glory is kavod and it speaks of a weight or a heaviness. It was that kind of glory that came when Smith prayed as well as in 2 Chronicles 5:14 where the priests could no longer perform their services. They were incapacitated because of the weighty glory!

As I mentioned in the introduction, no one knows for sure how much the actual Ark weighed (although, while researching online I found a vast variety of opinions ranging from hundreds to thousands of pounds). It was made of acacia wood and gold - with two gold cherubs on the top of the mercy seat. It also had the stone tablets of the Ten Commandments inside which would definitely contribute to its weight. What's the point? Whether it was hundreds or thousands of pounds, there was a weight to it, just like the glory of God. The priests felt the literal weight of the Ark on their shoulders. Remember, this book is about what God wants to form in us so we can carry the weight of who He is upon us.

Imagine the four to twelve priests distributing the weight of hundreds, if not thousands of pounds on their shoulders as they carried the Ark. I'm sure it wasn't easy and I'm sure it took some time to learn how to walk together with all that weight. There are many implications to us in this - the power of unity and community as we host God's Presence, learning how to literally keep "in step" with or walk in the Spirit, living with a daily awareness of God's Presence, and the obvious reference to the strength required to stand up under the weight of the Ark. The latter being the focus - yet all of those implications calling for acclimation.

I've fallen out in the Spirit while leading worship and and while preaching. Apparently I wasn't acclimated to the glory that was being poured out on me. But I was asking for it so praise God He answered.

Sometimes God just wants to take you down and do something in you, but other times He's inviting you to a greater measure of glory.

In doing that, He begins to pour out more until your spirit and body can handle it. Then instead of falling out every time, you can carry that new measure and walk in it. New strength is developed and now you can release a greater measure of glory in and through your life. It doesn't have to happen that exact way, but bottom line is, God wants to increase the measure of glory on our lives and that takes acclimation.

The more time you spend with God also acclimates you. Repentance, surrender, hunger, impartation, and faith are all keys. As we keep pressing in to the glory of the Lord, we get stronger in spirit and are able to handle more glory. Just like the young servants who would literally carry royalty on their shoulders with the palanquins, or the Levitical priests carrying the Ark - both requiring physical strength - it requires spiritual strength to carry a weightier measure of the King of glory on your life. This is what this whole book is about - being fit to carry the King.

BLESSED TO BE A BLESSING

"I will make you a great nation; I will bless you And make your name great; And you shall be a blessing." (Genesis 12:2)

God told Abraham that He would bless him and that Abraham would be a blessing. Through the new covenant, we have been given the blessing of Abraham (Gal. 3:14) so that now we are blessed to be a blessing. We are not just blessed, we *are* a blessing. We carry the Presence of God! We carry the blessing! The ark brought the blessing to Obed-Edom's house and now we carry the ark and the blessing everywhere we go.

Obed-Edom wasn't the only guy who experienced the blessing that the Presence of God brings. Joseph was a man who literally prospered everywhere he went, regardless of circumstances, because the Lord was with him (see Genesis 39). As a slave he prospered. As a prisoner he prospered. As a leader in Egypt he prospered. The only reason the scripture gives as to why he prospered was that "the Lord was with him." That's the blessing that the Presence of the Lord brings.

Psalm 91:9-10 says "Because you have made the LORD, who is my refuge, Even the Most High, your dwelling place, No evil shall befall you, Nor shall any plague come near your dwelling." Darkness and sickness are swallowed up in the glory of God. We see that demonstrated in Jesus' life.

Glory attracts blessing! My friends in Half Moon Bay, CA have a powerful church experiencing a move of the Holy Spirit. The pastor was telling me that from the start of the outpouring, finances began coming in an unexpected way. It was to him as if the offerings were being multiplied! That's Proverbs 10:22, "The blessing of the Lord makes one rich, and He adds no sorrow with it." By the way, you don't have to feel sorry for being blessed!

As Carriers of the Ark, this is all a sampling of what you are carrying! Perpetual springtime, weighty glory, healing, supernatural protection, freedom, deliverance, truth that sets free and the blessing of the Lord are all found in the Presence of God. Not to mention the unique anointing and calling God has placed on your life!

Since you are carrying the Ark, you have become a blessing everywhere you go. All of the blessing that you see throughout the Bible because of the Presence is now available through us. We are atmosphere shifters and glory carriers. When we show up, the blessing of the Lord comes with us. Businesses have the potential to prosper just because we are there. I'm partly joking when I say that restaurants get blessed when I show up. I'll walk in to Chipotle, for example, and there'll be no line at the register. Then within moments I turn around to see a big line forming behind me. What just happened? The business just got blessed because I came in as a blessing!

As You Go Lifestyle

I said all that because I want you know what you are carrying and who accompanies you. God wants to release a fresh boldness to bring His Presence in the public places. When I first heard about youth releasing the kingdom in malls and shopping areas, I was jealous! Bethel Church in Redding, CA as well as the ministry of Jesus Culture had activated young people in the gifts of the Spirit for evangelism. They took to heart the prayer that Jesus taught "on earth as it is in heaven." When youth in high schools were doing more than me in regards to outreach I knew something had to change! I was provoked for more.

We started doing what we called "prophetic dinners." When my friends and I would eat at restaurants we started asking the Lord for words He'd like to say to the servers. On one occasion, the group of young adults I was leading went to Denny's to eat after service. We all begin asking the Lord for words to share. When the server came back, we began to speak to her and she was getting ministered to prophetically! One of the young adults got a word of knowledge for pain in her foot and when we prayed she totally got healed. Then I asked her if she knew she was going to heaven and she wasn't sure so my wife and I led her to Jesus right there while she was on the job!

This was all new and exciting to us. We were carrying the life giving Presence of Jesus with us and people were getting impacted. The Lord spoke to me from Matthew 10:7-8 which basically says "as you go, release the kingdom." I knew it wasn't about an event mindset; it was about a lifestyle of releasing the kingdom of God "as you go." As we live our day to day lives, we could minister the love and power of Jesus to people.

Since then, we've seen many people get touched by God outside of the church. I was doing a prayer walk on the campus dorms that are next door to my church and I ran into one of the students that came to our group. She asked if I would come and pray a blessing over her sisters who had just dropped her off. I followed her to the parking lot and after greeting them began to pray. The Lord just said "healing" and highlighted a lower back. I prayed and one of the sister's backs got healed. Then another sister's arm got healed of an injury that caused limited mobility. She, being a dance instructor, needed to move! Then the third sister received healing from asthma! The best is their faces when they realize they're healed. They were pleasantly surprised at the goodness of God.

All of this happened unintentionally. I was just walking and praying, not intending on ministering to people. In Acts 3, Peter and John were just on the way to a prayer meeting when they had a divine appointment with the man at the Gate Beautiful. The man was crippled since birth and was radically healed in the name of Jesus. Can you imagine if the apostles just thought, "We can't stop right now, we've got to go pray" when the answer to a massive breakthrough in their city was sitting right there?! Thousands of people came to Jesus because of their willingness to live the "as you go" lifestyle!

One time my wife and I were in the drive through of the best burger place, In-N-Out Burger! I looked over and saw a bunch of gangster looking people sitting outside on the tables eating. I thought to myself, "What if I preached the gospel to them and they all got saved?" I went on and ordered, then the Lord said, "Why don't you do it?" I was freaked out! I didn't want to get stabbed for preaching the gospel!

I tried to shake it off, but the Lord kept on me. Then a Bible verse popped in my head. It's the second to last verse in Acts 5 and in summary says that the apostles were rejoicing because they were counted worthy of suffering for the name of Jesus. They just got beaten for preaching the gospel and were rejoicing. I'm thinking, out of all the verses to be brought up right now, that one Lord?! Maybe something like "I can do all things" or "The Holy Spirit is the Comforter"...nope. They rejoiced because they got beaten for Jesus. Ok, Lord, I get it. I've got to do this anyway.

I parked the car and my wife and I walked over to them. I told them I was just in the drive thru and God wanted me to come over here and tell you that He loves you. Right then, about three of them got up and were angry. One of them said, "We don't want to hear this!" Oh boy, here comes the knife! But actually they just walked away and I had a captive audience.

I preached the gospel to them all - Jesus died for them on the cross and wanted to forgive their sins. He wanted them to have a home in heaven and start a relationship with them today. Simple. My wife shared her testimony. She had more boldness than me for sure. Then I asked them if anyone would like to accept Jesus and a couple guys slowly put their hands up. So I said, "How about this. If you want to accept Jesus just come up here."

Everyone literally got up off the seats and formed a single file line in front of us to give their lives to Jesus! We had an altar call in the front of In-N-Out Burger and 13 people accepted Jesus! Hallelujah!

I guess my random thought of them all getting saved wasn't so random after all! As soon as we were done ministering, the angry group came back. God bound the enemy from messing anything up until the rest of the group gave their lives to Jesus. God is so good.

There are encounters waiting on the other side of your boldness. The one thing I've had to do more than anything else in order to see God touch people in the public places was take a risk. I really didn't know what was going to happen when I was going to preach to those people. I had to risk it. And the verse Jesus gave me wasn't giving me any excuse to back down - even though I wanted to! We've had people reject us and not want to hear what we have to say. They've turned down prayer. And we're still alive and ok! We still belong to a loving Father.

I believe God wants to stir you for bringing the power and love of Jesus to people in your day to day life. He wants you to live the "as you go" lifestyle. You carry the most powerful Presence in the universe! People have got to experience Him. We are portable Presence carriers.

TRAINING GROUND FOR WORLD CHANGERS

We need the local church. It's training ground for world changers. The fivefold ministers spoken of in Ephesians 4 are all given to the church to equip the saints for the work of ministry. In other words, church should be a place where we are equipped and trained to live like Jesus in all areas of life. The prophets should teach the people how to prophesy and the evangelists should teach the church how to evangelize and so on. Each of the fivefold ministers (apostle, prophet, evangelist, pastor and teacher) all carry a distinct aspect of Jesus' nature.

When we receive from all five, we become well rounded believers. When we miss out on one of the graces given to the church by Christ, we can be lop sided in regards to our Christlikeness.

That being said, God has provided for all of the training for the public place in the government of the church! As I grew in the local church, my pastor knew of the graces on his life and also knew where we needed to bring other fivefold ministers to equip the people. We would have training seminars, guest speakers and encounter nights for all kinds of things like prophecy, marriage, relationships, and missions. Through that and basic discipleship we all grew in maturity as followers of Jesus.

It's weird to me when people say that we don't need the church anymore. That's like saying a football player doesn't need to go to practice but he still wants to play in the game. Obviously if there is an abusive situation then it's time to find another church, but it's not time to give up completely on church.

Many people leave because of offense but what we don't realize is that offenses will come - especially in church! I actually believe it's God's way of bringing things to the surface that need healing in our own hearts. Church isn't perfect but it's God's perfect plan to grow people.

I've heard some interesting reasons for people not wanting church. One person told me that it's ok because they still have fellowship. But they never mentioned "I still have leadership." We need leaders! Many get offended with church leadership and end up leaving because they don't agree with how the leader runs things. It's probably true that the leader could do things better.

What if God was trying to teach you how to follow even when you don't agree? So that when God asks you to preach the gospel to a seemingly dangerous group of people (like me!), you know what it is to submit to a will that is not your own. In that, trust and submission are developed in your heart. Those are valuable virtues that Jesus walked in as a Son in relationship to His Father.

What does all this have to do with carrying the Presence?

Church is where you are trained in all of this stuff! I learned how to pray for people in church. I learned how to prophesy in church. I learned how to heal the sick, steward the Presence, love people, forgive people, treat people with dignity - all in church! It's where you should be trained in the lifestyle of Jesus.

It may not even look like the "normal" structure or style of most churches. What's most important is that we have God ordained leaders in our lives, peers we are walking with and people we are pouring into.

Having a local church or ministry that you're a part of gives you a place to "practice" ministry in a safe environment. Hebrews 5:14 (NASB) says, "But solid food is for the mature, who because of practice have their senses trained to discern good and evil."

Conferences, schools of ministry and bible colleges are all helpful

EVENTS ARE CATALYST TO LIFESTYLE

Being a part of a local church or ministry, you are most likely going to have outreach focused events. We want to reach our communities and the world with the gospel. Big events are important and necessary, but I also think that events are catalysts for a lifestyle. We don't want to turn the Presence carrying mindset on during an event and then once the event is over go back to "normal" whatever that is. Our normal should be constantly transforming into the normal lifestyle of Jesus. If our lives were to be inserted into the Book of Acts (cultural differences aside) would we be considered abnormal or normal Christians?

When we'd do outreach on the campus by my church, like I was mentioning before, I wouldn't know what I was about to say many times. I would start with small talk many times until God showed me something to speak, many times it being the slightest impression or just one word that I would use as a springboard to prophesy. My friend and prophet Jojo Henson said that prophecy is like a tissue box. You grab one tissue and the next one pops us right after it. When you're faithful to speak the first word God gives you, the next word will come. Psalm 81:10 says, "...Open your mouth wide, and I will fill it." I had to trust that when I opened my mouth, God would speak through me.

Later on I heard the general Mahesh Chavda say "The glory is always broadcasting." It was then I realized that if I can tap into God's frequency, I can hear His thoughts and share them as He leads me. Psalm 139:17-18 speaks of the innumerable thoughts that God has towards us and compares them to the sand on the seashore. This means that there's an unlimited amount of things that God is thinking about any one individual. In other words, there's not a shortage in God's mind on good things to encourage people with. He knows every detail of our lives, where we live, where we were born, our deepest pains, our greatest joys, our greatest potential, our unique personality, His plan for our lives, the gifts He put in us, and the right paths to take for us to prosper. Friendship with God means He begins to share His thoughts with you.

This is greater than just a weekend event! This is destiny launched out of intimacy. This is friendship with God that finds its way into your day to day life. People everywhere you go have the potential to encounter the love and power of Jesus - your neighbors, parking attendants, store clerks, people in line near you, servers, barbers, etc.

JUST BE NORMAL

One of the funny things we would come across when we started doing "prophetic dinners" was how serious everyone would get when they were listening for words for the server. We would be joking, having fun, snacking on appetizers and then all of a sudden a wave of silence would hit the table and everyone would get in soaking mode. Imagine the server coming back to what looked like a meditation center!

Just be you and just be normal. Be loving, be real, be respectful. You're not there to prove why they're "wrong". You're there to display Jesus and preach the gospel. The Holy Spirit will do the heart work. It's important to learn to communicate without being religious. You don't need to change your tone, volume, or accent in order for it to be anointed.

I remember hearing prophet Charlie Robinson share about how he worked in the public school system in Canada for years. He was in what would be a continuation school for troubled kids in high school. For example, one of the kids was arrested and the police found 26 handguns under his bed. It was such a potentially dangerous situation that the other teachers sat at their desk behind plexiglass for protection.

Charlie prayed in tongues around his desk and asked God to release

His glory. The glory of God would rest all around him. He noted that the kids would open up when they felt loved and could sense when people were being real. Once, a burly young man with tattoos came up to him in front of the class and asked, "How come it feels good right here? Not over there, or over there (pointing to other places in the room) but right here?" Charlie asked what it felt like. The young man responded, "It's like I'm stoned but I'm not." That young man felt the Presence of the Most High!

A young girl came up once and asked if she could sit near his desk for 10 minutes and get some peace before she went home. He recalled that he once had seven kids sitting around his desk because they enjoyed and received life from the glory emanating around him. The tough kids that many were afraid to deal with changed when the life giving Presence of Jesus manifested.

LOVE, TESTIMONY, POWER

"And now abide faith, hope, love, these three; but the greatest of these is love." (1 Corinthians 13:13)

God is love. His atmosphere is love. Friendship with God forms a heart that loves people. Loving people looks like seeing the best in them, even in enemies. The Presence isn't prejudice. Jesus gave life and acceptance to the "sinners" and prostitutes of His time. If we knew how God feels about the people around us, our hearts would overflow with love and kindness. His proof of love is His sacrifice at the cross. This kind of love is the bedrock and launching point for this entire chapter.

When my wife shares her testimony, she tells how she used to hate people. It's near unbelievable when you know who she is. But starting at an early age, many friends and important people that she loved moved away leaving her feeling abandoned. She didn't want to open up to anyone anymore if they were just going to move away. As a result, she ended up developing a hatred for people and a cynical outlook on life. She had a bit of a falling away from the Lord and found herself in a relationship that was unhealthy and ungodly. She knew she had to get back to Jesus.

It was then that she started going back to the church she was raised in. It just happened to be at the same time that I started going to that same church. She felt the Presence of God and His love captured her. After she surrendered her heart back to the Lord, God began to heal her view of people and began a process that opened her heart up to trust again. I know people who, on their first time visiting our church, met her, and testify to her being one of the first people they experienced unconditional love through. It's the love of God that changes lives.

I love how the palki, in ancient Indian culture, was accompanied by storytellers.[4] That's who we are. As we carry the King in on our shoulders, we get to testify of what He's done. What great feats He has accomplished. What great humility and mercy He's demonstrated. What power He's wrought by His mighty hand. How He has rescued us with a love that's incomprehensible.

Everyone has a story to tell. You've heard mine, you've heard my wife's, you've heard many others. But you have a testimony. How have you come to know Jesus? How has He touched your life? The thing about your testimony is that it's raw evidence of the reality of God. Your life becomes a living testament of the gospel. When the Woman at the Well shared her testimony, an entire city came to Jesus (John 4). If you're wondering where to begin when ministering to people, you always have your testimony.

Never underestimate the power of the gospel. Paul said, "For I am not ashamed of the gospel of Christ, for it is the power of God to salvation for everyone who believes, for the Jew first and also for the Greek." (Romans 1:16). He said the gospel is actually *the* power of God. The message of God's love coming to rescue mankind by giving His life on the cross has power within it. The Holy Spirit loves to come and confirm the gospel. In Acts 10:43-44 the Holy Spirit interrupted Peter's preaching and fell on all the people of Cornelius' house. The message of the gospel is of utmost interest to the Spirit of God!

You are a carrier of the life giving Presence of Jesus and the powerful message of the gospel. You have a story to tell. You carry the King in and the atmosphere comes under attention. You are not only blessed, you are a blessing.

I commission you to carry His Presence and bring the Bright and Morning Star everywhere you go, as you go! You are a Carrier of the Ark!

Questions:

- How have you seen God move supernaturally in or through your life?
- How have you acclimated to greater measures of the glory of God?
- When's the last time you took a "risk" for Jesus?

Activations:

- Have a prophetic dinner. Ask the Lord for words for your server and see what He does!
- Share your testimony with someone you don't know.
- Pray for someone in public (outside of your home and church).

Declarations:

- I am a risk taker for Jesus. I am as bold as a lion.
- I carry the Presence of God on my life. I shift atmospheres.
- I am not only blessed, I am a blessing.
- I help people encounter God.
- Even if people reject me, I'm still accepted by God.
- I have a story to tell because Jesus has moved in my life.
- I am naturally supernatural.

Endnotes

1   https://www.jewishvirtuallibrary.org/the-ark-of-the-convenant
2   https://www.sefaria.org/Sotah.35a?lang=bi
3   https://adventure.howstuffworks.com/outdoor-activities/climbing/
mount-everest6.htm
4   https://artsandculture.google.com/exhibit/human-powered-sedans-the-sto-
ry-of-palanquins%C2%A0-heritage-transport-museum/IAIy535Ha2n-Kw?hl=en

EPILOGUE

"And the things that you have heard from me among many witnesses,
commit these to faithful men who will be able to teach others also."
2 Timothy 2:2

The Ark wasn't meant to be carried on the shoulders of one, but of many. This means we've got to multiply! Jesus told us in the Great Commission to teach people to observe all that He commanded us. Freely you've received, freely give. It's time to give it away! We need multitudes of people carrying the Presence of Jesus in their day to day lives.

A few months ago, the Lord brought me back into the vision I shared about the two generations standing on the shore waiting for the next wave. The older man came to me and shook my hand and said, "You got this."

We are surrounded by a great cloud of witnesses of past generations cheering us on to fulfill the purpose of God in our day. May we be like David, who "after he had served the purpose of God in his own generation, fell asleep..." (Acts 13:36 NASB). Before we leave this earth, we will fulfill all that God wants to accomplish in our generation!

You got this.

RECEIVE JESUS

If you made it to this page, and aren't sure of where you'll spend eternity, please keep on reading.

Everything in this book is meant to point you to the relationship you can have with God through Jesus Christ. You were created by God, you are loved by God and you are called by God.

The issue is that we've all sinned and are in desperate need of a Savior. Our sin has separated us from God, distorted our view of Him, as well as, distorted our view of ourselves and our purpose. Yet, in the midst of our failures and distorted views, the good news still stands:

"For God so loved the world that He gave His only begotten Son, that whoever believes in Him should not perish but have everlasting life." (John 3:16)

The perishing has to do with us being disconnected from God, but isn't it amazing He loved us enough to make a bridge back to Him? He gave Jesus to make a way for us.

When Jesus came, He demonstrated the heart of God towards us - His teachings, miracles, healings, and example. The pinnacle of His life, however, was when He gave His life at the cross for us. The Bible teaches that the wages of sin is death (Rom. 6:23) so when Jesus died, He bore upon Himself the death we deserved for our sins. He dealt with what was separating us and became a bridge back to God.

All because of love.

He rose from the grave after three days dead and proclaimed victory over death and sin!

We all need saving and that's exactly what Jesus does. At this very moment, you can receive forgiveness of sins, have a home in heaven for eternity - and most of all, begin a right relationship with God, which is what you were created for!

I want to invite you to accept Him as your Savior.

You can pray something like this:

Lord Jesus,

I come to You now. I ask You to forgive me. I believe You died on the cross for my sins, You were buried, and on the third day, You rose again. Come into my heart. I make You my Lord and my Savior. This day, I receive Your forgiveness. Thank You for loving me, choosing me and giving me a brand new start. Fill me with Your Holy Spirit and empower to live this life for You.

In Jesus name, amen.

If you prayed this prayer, please let us know! We want to celebrate with you and send you a free gift.

Email us at: info@breakerministries.com

Find a good Bible believing, Holy Spirit filled, Jesus glorifying church to attend. This way, you'll be able to grow and connect with others who share the same faith. The best is yet to come!

BE FILLED WITH THE HOLY SPIRIT

"I am going to send you what my Father has promised; but stay in the city until you have been clothed with power from on high." *(Luke 24:49)*

Some of Jesus' last words before He ascended into heaven were to wait until they were clothed with power from on high. He was speaking of the Holy Spirit that would empower them to be witnesses for Him (Acts 1:8).

Jesus basically said don't go into all the world until you have supernatural power from the Spirit of God. If the disciples who literally walked with Jesus couldn't fulfill the call of God on their lives without power from on high, how much more do we need the Holy Spirit?

The life of Jesus is a supernatural life. He's called us to live naturally supernatural as we follow Him. A question that I've asked myself before is: "If I were to insert my life into the book of Acts, would I be a normal or abnormal Christian?"

The supernatural power of God was normal to the early believers. Healings, miracles, visions, prophecies, the gifts of the Spirit, and the help of angels were all normal. In fact, Jesus said Himself that those who believe in Him would do what He had been doing and even greater works! (John 14:12).

This all comes through the power of the Holy Spirit.

I want to invite you to receive the baptism of the Holy Spirit. To baptize means to be fully immersed in. God wants to clothe you with supernatural power.

One of the signs that you've been clothed and fully immersed in this power is the gift of speaking in tongues. Jesus said it's available to all who believe (Mark 16:17). It's a supernatural language that God gives you that has amazing benefits to your walk with Christ.

If you want to be clothed with this supernatural power, you can open your hands and pray something like this:

Father God,

I need Your power. So Jesus, baptize me with the Holy Spirit. Come Holy Spirit and fill me up. Clothe me with power from on high. I receive the gifts of the Spirit and the supernatural nature of God.

In Jesus name, amen.

Now just let Him fill you.

You may begin speaking in a new language. Just let it flow. Receive power from on high in Jesus name.

You may begin to see visions, hear the voice of God amplified, or just physically feel God coming upon you. I bless what God is doing in your life, in Jesus name.

Just wait upon Him and let Him move in your life.

If you prayed this prayer, please let us know! We want to hear how God moved and send you a free gift.

Email us at: info@breakerministries.com

ABOUT THE AUTHOR

Andrew Hopkins is a prophetic worship leader, revelatory preacher and teacher, and moves in the supernatural. He worked at his local church for over a decade in various pastoral positions and currently heads up his own itinerate ministry, Breaker Ministries. He also works at Elisha Revolution, with Jerame & Miranda Nelson as Worship Director and Associate Revivalist. Andrew earned a Bachelor degree in Christian Studies in worship from Vision International University. He and his beautiful wife Rochelle have two boys, Hunter and Everett, and live in San Diego, CA.

Stay connected -

Web: breakerministries.com

Instagram: @breakerministries

Facebook: Breaker Ministries

Join our email list today and receive a FREE 7 day devotional on breakthrough praise and worship entitled "Expand Your Expression." Go to **breakerministries.com** to sign up!

SEND OUT YOUR ROAR EP
8 original songs that are sure to provoke passion for Jesus, stir up the Spirit of revival, and release encounter with the God of the Breakthrough.

AVAILABLE AT:
breakerministries.com
& all online music stores

ANDREW HOPKINS

SEND OUT YOUR ROAR EP

CPSIA information can be obtained
at www.ICGtesting.com
Printed in the USA
LVHW021629180520
655946LV00009B/1159

9 780578 672618